Money & MARRIAGE

A COMPLETE GUIDE FOR ENGAGED AND
NEWLY MARRIED COUPLES

MATT BELL

D1024552

NAVPRESS
Discipleship Inside Out™

Discipleship Inside Out™

NavPress is the publishing ministry of The Navigators, an international Christian organization and leader in personal spiritual development. NavPress is committed to helping people grow spiritually and enjoy lives of meaning and hope through personal and group resources that are biblically rooted, culturally relevant, and highly practical.

For a free catalog go to www.NavPress.com
or call 1.800.366.7788 in the United States or 1.800.839.4769 in Canada.

NAVPRESS and the NAVPRESS logo are registered trademarks of NavPress. Absence of ® in connection with marks of NavPress or other parties does not indicate an absence of registration of those marks.

ISBN-13: 978-1-61521-561-4

Cover design and photography by Faceout Studio, Lindsey Brunsman

This book is designed to provide accurate and authoritative information in regard to the subject matter covered. It is sold with the understanding that neither the author nor the publisher is engaged in rendering legal, accounting, or other professional services. If legal advice or other professional advice, including financial, is required, the services of a competent professional person should be sought. The author and publisher specifically disclaim any and all liability arising directly or indirectly from the use or application of any information contained in this book. Some of the anecdotal illustrations in this book are true to life and are included with the permission of the persons involved. All other illustrations are composites of real situations, and any resemblance to people living or dead is coincidental.

Unless otherwise identified, all Scripture quotations in this publication are taken from the *Holy Bible, New International Version®* (NIV®). Copyright © 1973, 1978, 1984 by International Bible Society. Used by permission of Zondervan. All rights reserved. Other versions used include: The Holy Bible, English Standard Version (ESV), copyright © 2001 by Crossway Bibles, a division of Good News Publishers. Used by permission. All rights reserved; the *Contemporary English Version* (CEV) copyright © 1995 by American Bible Society. Used by permission; and the King James Version (KJV).

Library of Congress Cataloging-in-Publication Data

Bell, Matt, 1960-
  Money and marriage : a complete guide for engaged and newly married couples / Matt Bell.
      p. cm.
  Includes bibliographical references.
  ISBN 978-1-61521-561-4
  1. Married people--Finance, Personal. 2. Newlyweds--Finance, Personal. 3. Finance, Personal--Religious aspects--Christianity. I. Title.
  HG179.B3727 2011
  332.0240086'55--dc22
                           2010041087

Printed in the United States of America

1 2 3 4 5 6 7 8 / 15 14 13 12 11

For Jude

Because of you, my life is richer than I ever imagined.

CONTENTS

CHAPTER 1   What Is It About Money?   9

PART ONE:
Decoding Each Other's Financial DNA

CHAPTER 2   Getting Personal   19

CHAPTER 3   Outside Influences: How Family, Personal
             Experiences, and Culture Affect Your Finances   35

CHAPTER 4   Inside Influences: How Your Temperaments
             Affect Your Finances   43

PART TWO:
A Ten-Step Action Plan for Financial Success

CHAPTER 5   Plan to Succeed   59

CHAPTER 6   Work Wisely   75

CHAPTER 7   Give Some Away   81

CHAPTER 8   Put Some Away   91

CHAPTER 9   Ruthlessly Avoid Debt   97

CHAPTER 10   Manage Your Credit Score   109

CHAPTER 11   Patiently Pursue Interest   115

CHAPTER 12   Build Walls of Protection   129

CHAPTER 13   Spend Smart on Housing   141

CHAPTER 14   Spend Smart on All Other Expenses   151

PART THREE:
Fostering Financial Oneness

CHAPTER 15 One in Love, One in Money   161

CHAPTER 16 Details, Details   171

CHAPTER 17 Get Organized   185

CHAPTER 18 What It's All About   193

Acknowledgments   203

APPENDIX A Recommended Monthly Spending Guidelines   207

APPENDIX B Recommended Housing Guidelines   211

Notes   213

Author   219

CHAPTER 1

WHAT IS IT ABOUT MONEY?

The love of money is a root of all kinds of evil. Some people, eager for money, have wandered from the faith and pierced themselves with many griefs.

1 TIMOTHY 6:10

If a person gets his attitude toward money straight, it will help straighten out almost every other area in his life.

BILLY GRAHAM

JUDE AND I RARELY had disagreements during the six months we dated. Then we got engaged and registered for wedding gifts. The first true argument we had was about what pattern of dishes to register for.

I was all about modern design. Think clean lines, simple, minimalist. My father was a design professor, and those were the characteristics of designs he preferred, so they became my preferences as well. It's what I liked in clothing, furniture, artwork, and, as I soon discovered, dishes.

Jude was all about classic design. Think flowing patterns and intricate details. A set of formal dinnerware rimmed in gold is on

<9>

prominent display in the living room of her childhood home.

I assumed we would have dishes similar to what I grew up using. Sturdy. Simple. Solid white. Jude assumed we would have dishes similar to what she grew up using. Delicate. Intricate. Floral. *Floral!*

We should have seen it coming. While we were dating, Jude had made some comments about my apartment. "Cold" and "Like a boardroom" were some her more memorable descriptors. If I had been paying attention, I would have noticed a distinct lack of any modern design in her apartment.

I suddenly realized that making decisions about what to buy—what style of house, furniture, and car Jude and I would own—might require letting go of all that I found familiar. It wasn't just about what pattern would stare up at me from the bottom of my cereal bowl each morning. It was the possibility that something else, possibly lots of things, in our home would have a floral pattern. I felt queasy.

I also realized that if we were having such a tough time spending *other people's money*—after all, we were registering for the gifts we wanted our family and friends to buy for us—what about when it came time to spend our own money?

Guess who won the battle of the plates? Let's just say that even after eleven years of marriage, should one of our dishes break, Jude will say, "Please try to look upset." Or, "You could have at least made an effort to catch that dish before it crashed to the floor."

Over the years, we have learned to laugh about our differences and to compromise. I've become a bit less minimalist (is that redundant?). Jude has taken several steps toward the modern side of the spectrum. But it has taken time.

DIFFERENT PERSPECTIVES = CONFLICT

I'm sure it isn't news to you that money is one of the most common sources of disagreement among spouses. It causes more fights than sex or household chores,[1] and conflict over money predicts divorce better than other topics of dispute.[2] Couples who disagree about finances at least once a week are over 30 percent more likely to divorce than couples who disagree about finances a few times a month.[3] Yet turning down the financial heat between men and women is not easy because we come at money from such different perspectives. Consider the following:

- Men and women have different spending priorities. When asked about their indulgences, men are much more likely to say electronics (54 percent versus 23 percent of women); women are more likely to say travel (43 percent versus 33 percent of men).[4]
- Men and women view money through different emotional filters. When asked which terms best describe their feelings about money, men are more likely to choose *confidence* (58 percent versus 44 percent of women). Women are more likely to pick *anxiety* (33 percent versus 18 percent of men), *apprehension* (26 percent versus 15 percent of men), and *confusion* (14 percent versus 8 percent of men).[5]
- Of those who closely follow business and finance news, 65 percent are men.[6]
- Men and women are interested in different financial topics. Men are more into investing (83 percent versus 70 percent of women) and entrepreneurship (54 percent versus 36 percent of women). Women prefer savings (79 percent versus 69 percent of men), frugality (67 percent versus 53 percent of men), and shopping (20 percent versus 10 percent of men).[7]
- Men tend to be more aggressive with money. When applying for a job, for example, men are four times as likely as women to ask for more money than what is offered to them initially.[8] Men are typically more comfortable taking on higher levels of risk. According to one survey, 66 percent of husbands labeled themselves the couple's bigger risk taker with money versus 31 percent of wives.[9]
- More women (47 percent) than men (30 percent) feel they lack

knowledge about investing, and fewer women say they enjoy investing (55 percent versus 69 percent of men).[10]

Given the previous findings about investing, it's noteworthy that men make more investment mistakes than women, and they make them more often. For example, men are more likely than women to allocate too much of their portfolio to one investment (32 percent versus 23 percent of women), buy a hot investment without doing any research (24 percent versus 13 percent of women), and trade securities too often (12 percent versus 5 percent of women).[11] There's even evidence that women hedge fund managers outperform their male counterparts, with one ten-year study showing average annualized returns of 9 percent for hedge funds managed by women versus 5.8 percent for those managed by men.[12]

- Men and women differ in how they depict their current financial situation. Women tend to believe their situation to be worse than it actually is, sometimes overstating how much they have in debt. Men are just the opposite, tending to believe their situation to be better than it actually is, often overstating how much they earn.[13]

- Lastly, men and women differ in their charitable giving, with women somewhat more likely than men to donate time and money.[14]

FINANCIAL OPPOSITES ATTRACT

As if these general differences in perspective don't make it difficult enough to manage money as husband and wife, researchers from Northwestern University and the Wharton School of Business at the University of Pennsylvania found that we tend to magnify the difficulty by choosing mates who are especially different than we are when it comes to spending money. The research, published in a paper titled

"Fatal (Fiscal) Attraction," examined the mate selections of tightwads and spendthrifts. Tightwads were defined as people who find spending money to be painful yet regret not spending more. Spendthrifts were defined as people who feel little pain when they spend yet regret spending so much.[15]

The researchers found that in moments of clear, rational thinking—before someone we're attracted to walks by—we are aware of the type of person who would be best for us: someone whose attitudes toward money are similar to ours. However, when it comes time to make a decision, we set aside rational thinking. Tightwads tend to marry spendthrifts, and vice versa. The more we dislike our own financial tendency, the more likely we are to marry our financial opposite.

At first glance, that makes sense and may even seem beneficial, or at least harmless. It can be fun to hang out with our financial opposite while dating. A guy who can't bring himself to spend much may enjoy receiving nice gifts from a woman with a loose hold on her purse strings. However, the researchers say that from "I do" forward, life with a mate who approaches spending and saving differently than we do often leads to more financial conflict and less marital satisfaction.

By the way, despite the stereotype, it isn't always the woman who's the spender. In about one-third of couples, the husband freely admits he's the one who parts with cash too easily.[16]

OUT OF TOUCH, OUT OF SYNCH

If engaged or newly married couples don't discuss and come to terms with their financial differences, they may end up living separate, even secretive financial lives. Consider the following research findings:

- Nearly two-thirds (60 percent) of married people do not know when their spouse plans to retire.[17]
- Some 44 percent say it's okay to keep financial secrets from their spouse.[18] The most common secret is credit card or other

debt.[19] As I was working on this book, I came across a question to a financial columnist from a wife whose husband of twelve years had just told her that he owed $68,000 on his credit cards![20]

- Thirty-six percent of men and 40 percent of women confess to lying to their spouse at one time or another about how much they spent on something.[21]
- More than 20 percent of married people agree with this statement: "I don't discuss how much I make with anyone, including my spouse."[22]
- While women have a fairly good feel for what financial issues are important to their husbands, husbands not so much. Only 27 percent of men believe that having the right investments is very important to their wife, whereas nearly half of women say it's very important to them. Just 45 percent of men think having money set aside for emergencies is important to their spouse, whereas 68 percent of women say it's important to them.[23]

But money does not have to be a source of conflict in your marriage, even if these stats strike fear in your heart because you realize you're about to marry—or already have married—your financial opposite.

A VISION FOR YOUR FUTURE

If you are reading this book together, you are on the road to making your marriage different. You can learn to use money in a way that minimizes financial disputes, contributes greatly to your marital happiness, and gives you a sense of deep joy and satisfaction. Whether you are engaged or newly married, the book in your hands is a guide to that type of experience.

The next three chapters will help you each understand where the other is coming from with regard to money. You'll see where each of you stands financially and then explore how you got to where you are. I will give you many questions to discuss. By talking about the various influences that have impacted your use of money, you will gain empathy for each other, identify potential sources of financial conflict, and better understand each other's financial strengths and weaknesses.

The rest of the book will guide you through more specific financial instruction and give you additional questions to discuss so that you can use money to work as a team in accomplishing your financial goals.

If you are marrying for the first time and do not have children but hope to at some point, your life will never be as carefree as it is right now. Use this time to get on the same page financially and implement the proven money-management process taught in pages ahead. When life gets more complicated, you'll be especially glad you did.

If you put the principles in this book into action, you will experience money as a great blessing in your marriage rather than the all-too-common source of stress and conflict. I say that with complete confidence because these are not my principles; they are timeless truths about money found in the Bible.

Jesus once told a parable of a wise and foolish builder.[24] The foolish builder built his life on a foundation of sand. When the rains came, the streams rose, and the wind blew and beat against that house, it fell with a mighty crash. The wise builder built on the rock-solid foundation of God's Word. No matter how fierce the storm, that house stood strong.

If you put God's timeless truths about money into practice, you will build your financial home on a foundation solid enough to withstand whatever storms come your way, have the best possible chance of accomplishing your financial goals, and have great freedom to hear and respond to whatever adventure God calls you to take.

PART ONE

DECODING EACH OTHER'S FINANCIAL DNA

CHAPTER 2

GETTING PERSONAL

I know, my God, that you test the heart and are pleased with integrity.

1 CHRONICLES 29:17

Life can only be understood backward, but it must be lived forward.

SØREN KIERKEGAARD

NO ONE ENTERS MARRIAGE with a clean financial slate. In order to minimize marital conflicts about money, you need to know where each other stands financially speaking. You need to know each other's financial habits, attitudes, and circumstances.

Divorce attorneys tell me that many of the financial problems that end up coming between couples could have been prevented or at least lessened through full financial disclosure prior to marriage and through ongoing financial transparency during marriage. I want to help you have these kinds of financial conversations, so in this chapter, I've highlighted some key bits of financial information you need to know about each other and given you questions to discuss. If you haven't had many financial conversations yet, use this information to begin now.

<19>

As you go through the exercises that follow and discuss your answers to the questions, keep in mind that you are sharing some of the most personal details of your lives with each other. If you learn something surprising or concerning, do not convey judgment or alarm, and do not try to fix each other. There will be plenty of instruction later in the book. For now keep the focus on simply exchanging information and gleaning insights into what led both of you to where you are today.

FINANCIAL NET WORTH

To get a snapshot of where you stand money-wise, each of you needs to fill out a Financial Net Worth Statement. (If you are already married, do the best you can to remember your individual assets and liabilities before you tied the knot.) There's a blank Financial Net Worth Statement on page 21 that you can copy and fill out, or you can download a full-sized form from my website at www.MattAboutMoney.com (click on the "Resources" tab).

In order to complete the Financial Net Worth Statement, put the current value of each asset you own in the "Value" column (if you own a car, for example, list the current estimated market value, which you can find at www.kbb.com). Then put the amount you owe on each item, if any, in the "Debts" column. For anything on which you are making payments, the current amount owed may be on your most recent statement or on an amortization table on your original contract. If you don't have that information, call your lenders. For credit cards, include balances on only the cards you do not pay off each month. Of course, some items, such as a savings account, have value but no debt. Others, such as credit card balances, have debt but no value. Once you have finished listing the values of each asset and the amount of debt you have, total the "Value" column and the "Debts" column and subtract total debts from total value. The result is your current financial net worth.

Financial Net Worth Statement for 20 _____

Item	Value	Debts
Cash		
Checking Account		
Savings Account		
Savings Account		
Retirement Account		
Retirement Account		
Education Savings Account		
Education Savings Account		
Other Savings/Investments		
Home		
Other Real Estate		
Vehicle 1		
Vehicle 2		
Life Insurance (cash value)		
Household Furnishings		
Jewelry		
Artwork		
Credit Card Balance		
Credit Card Balance		
Credit Card Balance		
Credit Card Balance		
Student Loan		
Student Loan		
Other		
Other		
Other		
Other		
Other		
Totals		
Net Worth	$ _____	

TALK IT OUT

Once you have determined your financial net worth, go through the following questions and discuss them together. You don't have to tackle all of these questions in one conversation. Take them topic by topic.

Income. Unless you're living off an inheritance, your income is your financial engine. So even though it's not listed on the Financial Net Worth Statement, it makes sense to start here.

How much do each of you make per year?

If you've been working for the same employer for at least a couple of years, what types of raises have you received?

Do you like the company you work for? Why or why not? Do you enjoy your coworkers?

Do you enjoy what you do for a living—is it your passion, your mission—or is it simply a means to an end?

Do you aspire to go further in your field? What would that look like? A promotion within the same company? A change to a different company? What will it require? More time? More schooling? Better job performance?

If you plan to switch fields, why? What would you rather do? What are you doing in order to make this change happen? Ideally, when would you like to make this change?

What do you expect to be earning in five years? Ten years? What are you doing about that? Will more education be necessary?

If you plan to have children, would you prefer to remain a two-income couple after your children are born, or would you prefer to have one of you stay home?

Savings. How much do you have in savings? I'm not talking about 401(k) plan money. I'm talking about savings in a bank or credit union, a money market account, a money market mutual fund, or perhaps a certificate of deposit.

What's the purpose of this money? Is it your emergency fund?

If you lost your job tomorrow, how long would your savings last?

Do you think you have enough in savings?

Do you have any other type of an emergency fund? Do you think of your credit cards or a home equity line of credit as your emergency fund?

Are you saving for any future purchases? If so, what are you planning to buy?

Investments. How much money do you think you will need for retirement? How much should you be investing each month?

How much money do you have in a retirement account, such as a 401(k), 403(b), or 457 plan or an individual retirement account (IRA)?

How is this money invested? If it is in mutual funds, what types of funds did you choose?

Why did you choose those investments? Did you select them on your own or did you work with an advisor?

How much money do you put into these accounts each month? Does your company match some of the money you invest? If so, how much? Are you contributing enough to receive the full match? If not, why not?

How much money do you have in non-retirement investment accounts? How is this money invested? Do you invest in individual stocks or mutual funds? What is the purpose of this money?

How well are you doing in the pursuit of your retirement goals?

Would you describe yourself as a conservative investor or a risk taker? Why do you think you have your particular risk tolerance?

How often do you check on your investments?

Do you own a life insurance policy? If so, is it a term or permanent life insurance policy? What is the death benefit? Why do you own this, and who is the beneficiary? How much do you pay for it each month?

Assets. If you own a home, condo, or townhome, when did you make the purchase? How much money did you put down?

What is it worth, and how much do you still owe on it?

What type of mortgage do you have? What is its interest rate? Is it a fixed-rate or adjustable-rate mortgage? If adjustable, how long will it be before the interest rate changes? Are you planning to sell your property before then? If the interest rate is fixed, is it a fifteen- or a thirty-year loan? What is your monthly payment? Why did you choose this type of mortgage?

Will you live in this home after the two of you get married? If not, where should you live? What type of home would you like to have in the future?

How much is your vehicle worth, and what do you owe on it? How long do you typically keep your vehicles?

Do you usually finance cars or do you pay cash? Why?

How important is a car to you? Is it transportation or something more? Will you need two vehicles after you get married?

Do you own any other assets of value—artwork, jewelry, a vacation home, a timeshare, a trust?

Debts. How many credit cards do you have?

How do you use credit cards? What do you purchase with credit cards?

Do you carry a balance on any of your cards? In other words, do you pay less than the full balance each month?

If so, how much total credit card debt do you have? How did you get into that debt? Did you go through a tough financial circumstance or did the debt build up through lifestyle spending?

If you are carrying a balance on your credit cards, how do you feel about that? How big a priority is it for you to pay off the balances, and what are you doing about that? Are you paying more than the minimum due each month? Are you still using these cards?

If you have an education loan, how much total education debt do you have, what is your monthly payment, and how long is the term? Are you past due or have you ever defaulted on a student loan?

Do you owe money to any relatives, the IRS, or any medical providers? If so, how did those debts come about? What are you doing about those debts?

Have you ever declared bankruptcy or lost a home to foreclosure or a short sale? What happened? How long ago was that?

If you have been married before, do you pay alimony or child support? If so, how much each month? Are you behind on any spousal or child support?

EXPERIENTIAL NET WORTH

Next, fill out separate Experiential Net Worth Statements. You'll find a blank statement starting on page 26 and free downloadable full-sized forms on my website. The Experiential Net Worth Statement is designed to capture uses of money that typically don't show up on a Financial Net Worth Statement. For example, while it's technically true that money you spend on a vacation is an expense, the experience may have built a lifetime of great memories. In that sense, it may legitimately be considered an investment.

My intention with this exercise is not to help you justify foolish expenses on various experiences. Putting a vacation on a credit card that you are still paying off is not an investment; it's a mistake. However, if you saved for a vacation and the experience truly did enhance your life, that expense added to your experiential net worth. Same thing with education. Taking on $100,000 of student loan debt to obtain a degree in a field where you're likely to earn $30,000 a year is not a smart move. However, spending an affordable amount to enhance your work-related skill set or to improve at a favorite hobby are ways to grow your experiential net worth.

Generosity is the first category on the form because giving money to support organizations or causes you care about is one of the most satisfying uses of money. This section is divided between faith-based charitable organizations and other charitable organizations. I want you to look at those two types of generosity separately, as I'll be sharing some specific guidance about generosity in chapter 7. List each organization to which you donated money last year, the total amount you gave, and the percentage of your gross income that represented. Next,

Experiential Net Worth Statement for 20 _____

GENEROSITY

Faith-Based Organizations	Amount Given
Subtotal	$ _____
Percentage of Gross Income	_____ percent
Other Charitable Organizations	**Amount Given**
Subtotal	$ _____
Percentage of Gross Income	_____ percent
Total Charitable Giving	$ _____
Total Percentage of Gross Income	_____ percent

VACATIONS

Destination:

Details (How long was the trip? Who did you go with? What did you do? What were some of your favorite/most memorable parts of the trip?):

Destination:

Details (How long was the trip? Who did you go with? What did you do? What were some of your favorite/most memorable parts of the trip?):

Destination:

Details (How long was the trip? Who did you go with? What did you do? What were some of your favorite/most memorable parts of the trip?):

Destination:

Details (How long was the trip? Who did you go with? What did you do? What were some of your favorite/most memorable parts of the trip?):

EDUCATION

Class/workshop/degree program:

Details (What course did you take? Why did you take it? How will you use what you learned? What were some of the most memorable/helpful ideas you learned?):

Class/workshop/degree program:

Details (What course did you take? Why did you take it? How will you use what you learned? What were some of the most memorable/helpful ideas you learned?):

Class/workshop/degree program:

Details (What course did you take? Why did you take it? How will you use what you learned? What were some of the most memorable/helpful ideas you learned?):

Class/workshop/degree program:

Details (What course did you take? Why did you take it? How will you use what you learned? What were some of the most memorable/helpful ideas you learned?):

OTHER

Other experience:

Details:

Other experience:

Details:

Other experience:

Details:

Other experience:

Details:

list the vacations you took last year. You don't have to include every trip; just capture the most memorable and meaningful ones.

Do the same thing with education. Did you spend money on any classes, workshops, or other educational experiences last year? Include any expenses you incurred for someone else's education on this form as well.

TALK IT OUT

Now exchange forms and look them over. Take turns talking about whatever questions you have, and then discuss the following questions.

Generosity. How do you decide how much money to give away?

Do you base your giving on a fixed dollar amount or on a percentage of income? If you base your giving on a percentage of income, what percentage do you give each year and why? How has this changed over time?

How did you select the charitable organizations you support?

Is generosity fun and easy for you or is it difficult? Why?

How much teaching about generosity did you hear in church or elsewhere while you were growing up? What do you remember being taught? Was that instruction motivating or did it turn you off?

Vacations. How did you choose where to go last year? How did the trip(s) compare with your expectations?

Did you travel first-class or low-budget?

How did you pay for the trips? Are you still paying for them in the form of credit card debt, or did you save enough money for the trip before traveling?

Education. What classes or workshops did you take last year and why?

Were they for your professional or personal development?

Did you cover the cost or did your employer?

Does your employer offer tuition reimbursement? Have you taken advantage of that benefit? Why or why not?

Other. What other memorable experiences did you have last year?

Out of all of the experiences listed on your Experiential Net Worth Statement, which ones gave you the greatest enjoyment? Were any not worth the price?

Thinking about the future, what other experiences would you like to have?

Are there organizations or causes you'd like to support or specific amounts you'd like to give away?

Are there some vacations you're dreaming about, courses you'd like to take, or degrees you'd like to earn?

Are you saving right now in order to invest in such experiences?

EMOTIONAL NET WORTH

The last type of net worth to look at is your emotional net worth, which is an assessment of how you feel about your finances. While emotional net worth is much more subjective than financial and experiential net worth, it's an important part of your overall financial picture. After all, a person could have a high financial net worth and still be feeling a lot of financial stress, just as a person with a low financial net worth could be very much at peace. To get a snapshot of how you feel about your financial situation right now, respond to the statements on page 32 (you can download separate forms from my website).

TALK IT OUT

Once again, exchange forms and take a look at how each of you answered the questions. Then go through the following questions and discuss them together.

What are the strongest and weakest components of your emotional net worth and why?

Would you say you generally feel at peace financially, or do you

Emotional Net Worth Statement for 20 _____

1. I argue about money with the people I care about.

   Never   Rarely   Sometimes   Often

2. I feel stressed about money.

   Never   Rarely   Sometimes   Often

3. I lose sleep because of financial concerns.

   Never   Rarely   Sometimes   Often

4. I feel unhappy because there's something I'd like to buy that I can't afford.

   Never   Rarely   Sometimes   Often

5. I feel envious about what other people own.

   Never   Rarely   Sometimes   Often

6. When my credit card statement arrives, I'm afraid to open it.

   Never   Rarely   Sometimes   Often

7. I worry about losing my job because I don't know how I'd pay my bills.

   Never   Rarely   Sometimes   Often

8. I stay current with wise money-management ideas by reading financial magazines, newspapers, and blogs or by listening to or watching financial programs.

   Never   Rarely   Sometimes   Often

9. I'm confident I'm saving enough.

   Not   Not   To Some   To a Great
   at All   Much   Degree   Degree

10. I make informed investment decisions.

    Not   Not   To Some   To a Great
    at All   Much   Degree   Degree

11. I believe I'm making a difference in the world with the money I donate.

    Not   Not   To Some   To a Great
    at All   Much   Degree   Degree

12. I know what to do to keep my credit score strong and am doing it.

    Not   Not   To Some   To a Great
    at All   Much   Degree   Degree

13. I have a sense of peace about money.

    Not   Not   To Some   To a Great
    at All   Much   Degree   Degree

14. My use of money is an expression of my highest priorities and commitments.

    Not   Not   To Some   To a Great
    at All   Much   Degree   Degree

15. I live with a sense of freedom with regard to money.

    Not   Not   To Some   To a Great
    at All   Much   Degree   Degree

Based on your responses, how would summarize your overall emotional net worth?

   Very   Somewhat   Somewhat   Very
   Weak   Weak   Strong   Strong

have some financial concerns?

If your emotional net worth is anything less than "very strong," what are you doing or what could you do to improve it?

In the interest of full financial disclosure, here are a couple of other topics you should discuss.

Budget. Do you use a budget? Why or why not?

If you use a budget, what process do you use? Is it on a piece of paper? An electronic spreadsheet? Budget software? An online tool? Why have you chosen this method of budgeting?

Would you describe your budget as detailed or general?

What have been the main benefits of using a budget? What have been some of the main challenges?

If you are not using a budget, how open are you to using one in the future?

Credit reports and scores. Pull your credit reports at www .annualcreditreport.com. Your credit reports are free; your credit score is not. There are some websites that offer free credit score estimates, but I recommend that you purchase your FICO score. FICO stands for Fair Isaac Corporation, which is the company that created credit scores and whose scores are the most widely used.

As I was writing this book, a bill was making its way through Congress that would make our credit scores available to us for free under certain circumstances. For the latest on that, check my website.

Currently, you can purchase your FICO score for $15.95 by going to www.myfico.com. You'll have your choice of purchasing your TransUnion FICO score or your Equifax FICO score. You cannot purchase your score from the third credit bureau, Experian, as it no longer sells its score to individuals. For now, it doesn't matter which one you choose; just buy one.

Credit scores range from 300 to 850. Unlike cholesterol, the higher the number the better. You'll get the best rates on a mortgage if your score is in the mid 700s or higher.

How do your scores compare? Does one of you have a much lower score than the other? If so, do you know what may be pushing your score down? Also, don't panic. In chapter 10, I'll have a lot more to say about how credit scores work and what you can do to improve your score and keep it strong.

GOING FURTHER

By now you probably know much more about each other's financial circumstances than you have in the past, and you know some of the thinking behind each other's financial decisions. Still, there are other important factors that have led you to where you are today and will continue to influence your financial beliefs and behavior in the future. We'll look at these in the next two chapters.

CHAPTER 3

OUTSIDE INFLUENCES:
How Family, Personal Experiences, and Culture Affect Your Finances

Do not conform any longer to the pattern of this world, but be transformed by the renewing of your mind. Then you will be able to test and approve what God's will is—his good, pleasing and perfect will.

ROMANS 12:2

In every conceivable manner, the family is link to our past, bridge to our future.

ALEX HALEY

FIVE MONTHS INTO THEIR dating relationship, Julie and Sam went to see the Chicago Cubs play at Wrigley Field. In the midst of an enjoyable outing, the topic of money came up. When Julie mentioned that she was carrying a $1,200 balance on a credit card, the flow of

<35>

conversation suddenly turned into an extended awkward silence. Sam remembers feeling stunned, like a batter hit by a hard curveball that seemed to come out of nowhere. To him, carrying a balance on a credit card was nothing short of irresponsible. Scrambling for something to say, he only made matters worse by offering to loan Julie enough money to pay off her balance. Julie felt judged.

As difficult as that conversation was, it ended up spurring more conversations that helped this couple learn more about the source of each other's financial habits and attitudes. Sam came from a stable, middle-class family. His dad was a college professor and made extra money in the summer painting houses. They lived within their means, always bought used cars, and saved diligently for their annual family vacation. They weren't rich, but they always had enough money in the cash drawer in the kitchen for groceries and other essentials. For most of his growing-up years, Sam's parents bought everything with cash. Julie jokingly says that Sam's family is right out of *Leave It to Beaver*, a sitcom from the fifties and sixties about an idealized suburban family.

Julie describes her own family as "somewhat more colorful." Her parents divorced when she was five. While her mom had a reputation for knowing how to stretch a dollar further than most, money was always tight. During the years between the divorce and Julie's leaving the nest, there was just one family vacation, a trip to Florida. Julie's mom still reminisces about it.

A few days after the credit card conversation at Wrigley Field, Julie told Sam of a time when she had to help her mom make her mortgage payment. Sam felt much more empathy. Julie also told him that she once had a balance of over $10,000 on credit cards and had paid it off before they met. Still, she felt comfortable carrying a balance and was in the habit of occasionally letting balances build up on her cards. She always found it manageable on her salary. However, as she learned more about Sam's upbringing, she understood why he hated the idea of carrying a credit card balance, and she quickly paid off her balance.

Today, after about a year of marriage, Julie credits those first conversations about money with leading them to a place of greater free-dom. "When we got married, there was nothing about our spending habits that we didn't know about each other."

Julie's and Sam's spending habits and attitudes were clearly influ-enced by how each of them was raised. This is true for all of us, so let's explore how your family, your personal experiences, and our culture have contributed to your current financial situation.

FAMILY

Our families impact the way we think about and use money in count-less ways. The problem is, we may not even realize how we have been affected. For instance, you might be extremely cautious with money because your great-grandfather lived through the Depression, and he passed his financial fears down to his daughter, and she passed them down to her daughter (your mother), and she passed them down to you. No one broke the cycle of fear by learning about diversification or asset allocation. You just remained stuck in the financial patterns set by your great-granddad so many years ago.

Sometimes just by talking about your family's history with money you can see where you got your financial philosophy. That can help you think about whether it's helping you or hurting you, and it just might create the motivation to choose a better path.

The following questions are designed to get the two of you talking together about how your families did the whole money thing:

How well did your parents deal with money? Did they struggle with money, or were they at ease with financial matters? Was money always scarce, or was it plentiful?

How often did they fight about money?

Did they give you an allowance? If so, starting at what age? Did you have to work for it, or did they just give you the money? How well did that system work?

Did your parents ever sit down and teach you about money? If so, what lessons did they teach? Did those lessons stick, or did you resist them?

Did your parents use a budget?

Were your parents generous or tight? Did they regularly give money to charitable organizations? If so, which ones? Did they seem to enjoy giving, or did they give out of obligation? Did they encourage you to give?

How frequently did your family go on vacations, and what types of vacations did you take?

How well did your parents tip when you ate at restaurants? Were you ever embarrassed at how little they left?

Were they jealous of others or happy for them? How often did they comment on other people's financial situations, such as the neighbor's new car or a coworker's recent vacation?

Did they feel entitled, or was it up to them to earn whatever they got?

Did both of your parents work while you were growing up? How did you feel about their work choices? If both of your parents worked, was that okay with you?

Were your parents steady in their careers, or did they change jobs frequently?

Do you think your parents worked too hard or not hard enough? Was either one a workaholic?

Who did the grocery shopping in your family? Was he or she a coupon clipper?

What types of stores did your family choose when shopping for clothing? Department stores, discount stores, outlets?

What types of cars did your parents drive?

How old were you when you got your first car? Did your parents buy it for you, or did you pay for it?

In what ways have these experiences impacted your financial views or habits?

Have you adopted your parents' ways of thinking about and

managing money, or have you taken the opposite approach? In what ways are you similar to your parents in how you think about and use money, and in what ways are you different?

Who else influenced you financially as you were growing up? Are there other family members or friends who had an impact?

Are there any dramatic money stories from your family's past? Did anyone go bankrupt? Make a million bucks?

In addition to our family, our experiences also influence our financial attitudes and habits. In this next section, you will explore what personal experiences have had the greatest impact on shaping your beliefs or behavior in regards to money.

PERSONAL EXPERIENCES

I was twenty-five when an uncle died and left me $60,000 in his will. I had no idea he planned to leave me any money. It was a complete shock. At the time, I was making about $25,000 per year working as a radio journalist. Think of your annual income and multiply that number by about two and a half, and you'll get a sense of how it felt to inherit that money.

I used the money to create my dream job: a newsletter for people who take golf vacations. At the time, golf and travel were two of my favorite hobbies, and I was trained as a journalist. I figured it would be a blast to spend my life visiting some of the world's greatest golf resorts, playing, photographing, and reviewing their courses. Because I had what seemed like an endless pile of money in the bank, it didn't concern me that I wasn't attracting many paid subscribers. I just kept going. Two years later, I had blown through the entire $60,000 plus another $20,000 on my credit cards. I went from living the life to living in my parents' basement for six months.

That was one of the most difficult, embarrassing, and humbling experiences I've ever been through. For the first two months at my parents' house, I was deeply depressed. Ultimately, though, the experience was used for good. It prompted me to take a much greater interest in spiritual matters and eventually commit my life to Christ. That financial tough time also got me interested in learning how to manage money well, something I've been studying ever since.

But the aftermath of that experience is more complex, and in some ways I still haven't fully come to terms with it. A couple of years ago, while telling a friend about the experience, I was surprised to find myself in tears. Even though so much good has come from that painful lesson, apparently I still have not forgiven myself for not doing a better job managing that money.

What about you? Has any major event shaped your view and use of money? What happened? How did it impact you initially, and how does it continue to impact you?

The final external factor to explore together is how our culture has influenced each of you when it comes to how you deal with money.

CULTURE

Our culture has a lot to say about money. Think of the advertising you see each day. What are the messages? Ads for new cars are usually not about how long the car will hold up; they're about how you will feel and how others will perceive you if you drive such a car.

What about the name used by the media and our political leaders to describe us? They call us consumers, right? That's the term we read in the paper and hear on the news all the time. Have you ever looked up the definition? "To consume" literally means to devour, destroy, use up, or spend wastefully. That explains a lot, doesn't it?

Consumers take their identity from what they own—the brand of clothing they wear, the type of car they drive. They look to possessions for much of their happiness, and their happiness is often relative. They feel happier when they get something more or when they see they have more than a friend, relative, or coworker has. As a result, they usually have too little money in savings and too much debt.

In reality, few of us are over-the-top consumers. However, most of us look at life to some extent through the filter of a consumer. To what degree do you think or act like a consumer?

Think of your colleagues and friends. Think of your neighbors. How often do you find yourself playing the comparison game? To whom do you most often compare yourself? What comparisons do you make? Do you compare brands of clothing? Cars? Vacations?

Who are some of the worst financial role models in your life—people who are clearly living as consumers and who negatively impact your financial habits?

Who are some of the most positive financial role models in your life—people who seem to be least affected by our consumer culture? What do you admire about the way they handle money? How have their decisions impacted your thinking and behavior regarding money?

CONTINUOUS LEARNING

Understanding how your family, your personal experiences, and our consumer culture impact your financial attitudes and behavior is not a onetime proposition. We all continue to be influenced by these factors, so continue to be on the lookout for any unhealthy ways they are at work in your life. And be gentle about pointing out how they may be at work in your spouse's life. If your mate works a lot of weekends, comments like "You're just like your dad" are not likely to go over very well. Questions such as "Who may have influenced you to work so many hours?" tend to work better.

Now let's move on to another factor that has a strong influence on how we manage money: our temperament.

CHAPTER 4

INSIDE INFLUENCES:
How Your Temperaments Affect Your Finances

For as he thinketh in his heart, so is he.

Proverbs 23:7 (KJV)

Solvency is entirely a matter of temperament and not of income.

Logan P. Smith, essayist

WHEN JUDE AND I met, I was a product manager at a market research firm. Right after we got engaged, I changed employers and got a nice raise, along with the potential to earn fairly sizeable bonuses. Jude was in her eighth year of working for Campus Crusade for Christ, a Christian ministry that works with college students. I was earning almost three times as much as she was making. Plus, I am eight years older than she is. Still, despite my higher income and longer amount of time to earn money, she was in better financial shape than I was. Jude had more money in retirement savings, owned a paid-off car that was two years newer than mine, and gave away a higher percentage of her income.

<43>

In part, these differences were because I had gone through a dramatic financial crash and burn while I was in my mid-twenties, as I described in the previous chapter. In essence, I had stood still financially for about seven years while Jude was making steady upward progress.

Even though she didn't earn a high income, Jude excelled at living within her means while setting money aside for the future. When we were dating, I never heard her complain about not having enough money for this or that. She was content. And it wasn't like she was wearing rags or anything.

In fact, here's one of my favorite stories about Jude's ability to live well on a little. One winter day she was walking along a fashionable street in downtown Chicago when a well-dressed, wealthy-looking woman stopped her and asked where she had purchased the leopard print hat she was wearing. I'm sure the woman was expecting Jude to name a store like Saks Fifth Avenue, Nordstrom, or Macy's. So imagine how taken aback she was when Jude explained she had picked it up—for free—at a thrift store where she was volunteering. Because the hat hadn't sold after several weeks in the store, it was about to be tossed in the trash and Jude snagged it.

I once asked her how she became so good at living within her means. She shrugged her shoulders and said, "Isn't that what you're supposed to do?" Her wise financial habits, and the fact that they come to her so naturally, can be explained, in part, by her temperament.

HOW GOD HAS WIRED YOU

Knowing your temperament and that of your fiancé/fiancée or spouse will open up a whole new window of understanding. It will go a long way toward explaining why you both do what you do with money (and everything else, for that matter). It can also help you manage money as a team while minimizing your financial disagreements.

The simple insight that a person's temperament typically does not change should help. If you're having recurring disagreements, maybe it's because you keep trying to change something about each other that won't ever change. That's not to say that temperament is an excuse to keep doing something that irritates your spouse. While we may not be able to change our temperament, we can learn to manage it. Becoming aware of how your temperament influences your attitudes and behavior is the first step toward being able to maximize your natural strengths while not being at the mercy of your natural weaknesses.

There are several different temperament classification systems, but they all have their roots in the one formulated by Hippocrates, the father of modern medicine, all the way back in 370 BC and then refined by the Roman physician Galen in 190 AD.[1] This system consists of four temperaments: choleric, sanguine, phlegmatic, and melancholy.

Each of us has a primary and a secondary temperament; let's find out yours.

IDENTIFY YOUR TEMPERAMENT

In order to determine your temperament, review the characteristics for each of the four temperaments in the chart on the following pages,[2] checking the box for each characteristic that describes you. As you'll see, some are positive characteristics and others are negative. Be as honest as possible in indicating whether you can relate to each one. When you are finished, add up the number of characteristics you checked for each section.

Temperament Chart

A

- ☐ Strong-willed, determined
- ☐ Time is most valuable asset
- ☐ Driving personality
- ☐ Impatient—wants it done yesterday
- ☐ Sometimes bossy
- ☐ Direct, forceful
- ☐ Values tasks over people
- ☐ Natural leader
- ☐ Likes to be in control
- ☐ Sometimes intolerant of others
- ☐ Decisive
- ☐ Strongly opinionated
- ☐ Independent, hard-working

- ☐ Self-motivated
- ☐ Confident
- ☐ Self-reliant
- ☐ Self-assured
- ☐ Goal oriented
- ☐ Aggressive driver
- ☐ Risk taker
- ☐ Prone to anger
- ☐ Sarcastic
- ☐ Argumentative
- ☐ Insensitive, unsympathetic
- ☐ Practical

B

- ☐ Talkative, popular
- ☐ Loud, sometimes brash
- ☐ Emotionally volatile at times
- ☐ Persuasive
- ☐ Quick-tempered
- ☐ Colorful, exciting personality
- ☐ Fun-loving
- ☐ Low self-control
- ☐ Impulsive
- ☐ Low sales resistance
- ☐ Compassionate
- ☐ Emotionally responsive
- ☐ Warm, friendly

- ☐ Outgoing, extroverted
- ☐ Enthusiastic
- ☐ Loves people
- ☐ Great encourager
- ☐ Not well organized
- ☐ Loves approval of others
- ☐ Restless
- ☐ Optimistic
- ☐ Sometimes late to appointments
- ☐ Not good at details
- ☐ Sensitive
- ☐ Not well-disciplined

C

- ☐ Calm, cool
- ☐ Laid-back
- ☐ Easygoing
- ☐ Quiet, reserved
- ☐ Inactive, sometimes lazy
- ☐ Tendency toward passivity
- ☐ Avoids and dislikes conflict
- ☐ Slow to make decisions
- ☐ Peaceable, peace loving
- ☐ Quick, dry wit
- ☐ Diplomatic in conflict resolution
- ☐ Dependable, reliable
- ☐ Objective

- ☐ Efficient
- ☐ Orderly
- ☐ Agreeable, likeable
- ☐ Hard to motivate
- ☐ Frequently waits until last minute
- ☐ Often indecisive
- ☐ Fearful, worrier
- ☐ Self-protective
- ☐ Saves everything
- ☐ Introverted
- ☐ Stubborn
- ☐ Works well under pressure

D

- ☐ Perfectionist
- ☐ Analytical
- ☐ Industrious
- ☐ Musically inclined
- ☐ Enjoys art, music, things of beauty
- ☐ Detail oriented
- ☐ Precise, exact
- ☐ Introspective
- ☐ Self-sacrificing
- ☐ Excellent planner
- ☐ Supportive of others
- ☐ Self-disciplined
- ☐ Serious

- ☐ Gifted, multi-talented
- ☐ Aesthetic
- ☐ Worrier, fearful
- ☐ Critical and picky
- ☐ Indecisive
- ☐ Pessimistic
- ☐ Deeply emotional, moody
- ☐ Creative
- ☐ Sensitive
- ☐ Loyal, faithful
- ☐ Frozen by fear, worry, depression
- ☐ Harbors resentment

Add up how many boxes you checked for each of the four sets of characteristics.

A _____ B _____ C _____ D _____

The one with the highest number is your *primary temperament type*. The one with the second highest total is your *secondary temperament type*. Here's the scoring key.

A = Choleric
B = Sanguine
C = Phlegmatic
D = Melancholy

Now let's look at some ways that each temperament may impact a person's financial beliefs and behaviors.[3]

THE CHOLERIC AND MONEY

General description. Hard-charging, bottom-line, type-A.

Financial implications. Cholerics are great at casting vision and barreling through any obstacles that stand between them and their goals. Direct that vision and perseverance toward a financial goal such as getting out of debt or saving for the down payment on a house, and look out. A choleric can charge right to the head of the money class. The only problem is, because of their aggressive, time-sensitive nature, cholerics often run ahead of their spouses, leaving them out of financial decisions, failing to share passwords to bank and investment accounts, and even making investments without talking about them beforehand.

Cholerics thrive on being productive, getting things done, and achieving results. They are often good providers but may be vulnerable to workaholism, which can be a threat to a marriage. According to one study, marriages involving a workaholic are twice as likely to end in divorce.[4] If your fiancé/fiancée or spouse overdoes the hours at work, experts recommend that you not enable that tendency by always re-arranging your schedule to accommodate his or hers. Also, find mutually enjoyable activities you can take part in together.

When planning a major purchase, especially if it's something they strongly desire, cholerics will do a good job at finding the best deals, as long as it doesn't take too long. That last part is especially important. I am primarily a choleric. I value getting a deal but I need it to be done quickly. Once cholerics know where to buy the item for the best advertised price, their assertive negotiating skills can generate additional savings. Just make sure not to browbeat the salesperson in the process; cholerics value tasks over people.

Cholerics do a good job of organizing their household's bill-paying system. Because they are typically organized and hate being late, they'll make sure bills are paid on time.

If you are married to a choleric and want your spouse to go with you on a shopping trip, don't expect him or her to revel in a leisurely stroll through the mall. Cholerics want to find what is needed and get out of there. You may be better off shopping separately.

Cholerics can be demanding of their spouse, wanting to see what he or she bought at the store and checking to see how much was spent. If you are a choleric, make sure your budget has a category for your non-choleric spouse to manage—at least his or her own clothing budget, and perhaps a budgeted amount for a hobby or lunches with friends. As long as your spouse stays within that amount, no rifling through clothing purchases or asking to see receipts.

Cholerics may be too aggressive in investments[5] and can fall for get-rich-quick schemes—all the more reason to consult your spouse before making that trade. Also, watch out for a tendency to hoard, as cholerics often find it easier to take their sense of security from their bank or investment accounts than from God.

Generosity may not come naturally to cholerics, unless they see the practical benefit. A choleric friend struggled with the decision to participate in his church's building campaign until the pastor specified the cost of each seat in the new sanctuary. Motivated by the tangible results of each dollar given, my friend ended up making a generous contribution.

Choleric pros/cons and what to do. Your action orientation can be a good thing. You'll position yourself for the next promotion, take full advantage of your employer's retirement plan, and not get stuck overanalyzing your insurance needs.

Your main watch-out is to not leave your spouse out of financial decision making. Add the following items to your ever-present to-do list: Give spouse access to the passwords, provide a summary of financial accounts owned, and schedule regular meetings to discuss investments and other financial decisions.

Bonus idea. Want to buy a choleric spouse a great gift? Choose something practical, utilitarian. Even better, give a gift card so he or she can choose the gift.

THE SANGUINE AND MONEY

General description. Outgoing, colorful, life of the party.

Financial implications. Sanguines are all about being with people, so they naturally gravitate toward and succeed in people-oriented jobs, such as sales. However, the combination of a variable income and a decided lack of interest in details can leave a sanguine's finances in a bit of a mess. Budget? Who has time for that? Sanguines would rather be out socializing. If you are married to a sanguine, don't try to turn your spouse into the keeper of the household budget. It isn't going to happen. Just get him or her to drop receipts in the vicinity of your budget, and then enter the data yourself.

Their focus on the present may also leave sanguines ill-prepared for future needs such as retirement or a child's college tuition. They are not the best at balancing their checkbook or paying bills on time.

Because they thrive on approval and like to be noticed, sanguines may overdo it on the latest fashions, vehicles (can you say, "Red sports car"?), or technology. Let's face it: They are not likely to get a lot of compliments driving an old car—or even a new beige one, for that matter—or wearing practical shoes.

Because they are more driven by feelings instead of facts, sanguines may make purchases without researching the best options, especially if there's a likeable salesperson involved. A tendency toward impulse purchases along with low sales resistance may make sanguines susceptible to coming home with big-ticket surprise gifts with all the extras, like a big-screen TV along with the priciest extended warranty. After all, the salesperson was such a great guy; he exuded trust.

When it comes to investing, sanguines are willing to take risks. However, because they usually don't take the time to create a well-thought-out investment plan, they can make bad investment decisions.

Sanguines are typically very generous, which can motivate a less generous spouse. However, their trusting nature can make them fall for fund-raising scams.

Sanguine pros/cons and what to do. Your fun-loving nature can help a frugal spouse learn to enjoy more of the things and experiences money can buy.

Your main watch-out is a tendency to overspend. One of the most practical steps you can take is to use an envelope system for budgeting. Once you are out of money in a particular category, that's all you can spend for the month. (I'll talk more about how to do this in chapter 5).

Because you tend to be very generous, which can lead to overspending on gifts, consider making things for people instead of buying them expensive things. Better yet, give them certificates for projects you will help them with. That'll give you an opportunity to spend more time with your friends without spending money.

Bonus idea. Want to buy a sanguine spouse a great gift? Throw a party in that person's honor and invite all of his or her favorite friends.

THE PHLEGMATIC AND MONEY

General description. Reliable, dependable, predictable.

Financial implications. Phlegmatics have a strong work ethic; they can be counted on to show up and methodically get the job done. However, a lack of motivation to reach for the next rung on the corporate ladder, combined with a preference to work behind the scenes, may leave them performing below their career potential.

Phlegmatics tend to be organized and good planners; it's follow-through that's the problem. They may do a fine job with hanging on to their receipts but never get around to developing a budget. They have all the details of their financial life; they just don't have a compelling vision for where they want to go.

They sometimes wait until the last minute to pay bills or file taxes. They're the ones you see on TV putting their tax returns in the mailbox on April 15.

Phlegmatics are good at living within their means. They are excellent bargain shoppers, possibly leaning toward being cheap. They are content to drive older cars, eat in inexpensive restaurants, and stay in budget hotels when vacationing.

Because they don't like spending money, they might find tipping to be a challenge. You know you're a phlegmatic if you have a laminated tip card in your wallet that tells you exactly how much to leave your server and if you rarely leave more than 15 percent. This reluctance to spend may also make it a challenge to give money to charitable organizations. However, phlegmatics are also empathetic, so once they see a clear need, they can be generous.

They have a hard time throwing things away, even if clothing is out of fashion or the sofa is threadbare. If your closets, garage, or basement are packed with stuff, you may be phlegmatic.

Phlegmatics may agree to their need to start saving or investing but then put it off. Once they get started, though, they are good at sticking with the plan.

They are patient and persistent, although they can be overly conservative, especially with investments. They prefer bonds over stocks. However, because of their rational bent, they have the potential to choose well-researched investments. They may just need their spouse to help them pull the trigger on the investment once the research is done.

Because they avoid conflict, phlegmatics have a hard time contacting their creditors when in financial trouble. But once they solve their problem, they are unlikely to get into trouble again.

They are slow to make decisions, preferring to know all of their options. This can drive a choleric spouse crazy, but once a phlegmatic decides, they tend to make good decisions.

Phlegmatic pros/cons and what to do. Your ability to live within your means will serve you and your spouse well. It's an unusual trait in our marketing-saturated, consumer culture.

Your main watch-out is to not let frugality turn into cheapness. A sign that you may have moved into the cheap camp is when your money-saving ways damage relationships. If you are a phlegmatic husband, for example, you may need to overcome some internal resistance to buying your spouse gifts from time to time—and I mean something other than what you find in the bargain bin.

Bonus idea. Want to buy a phlegmatic spouse a great gift? Buy a high-quality version of something he or she enjoys. If your spouse likes to garden, for example, but uses rusty tools picked up at garage sales, buy him or her a new set of hand tools.

THE MELANCHOLY AND MONEY

General description. Disciplined, likes to plan, has lofty ideals.

Financial implications. Of all the different temperament types, melancholies are the most likely to enjoy using a budget. Their detail orientation makes them good at keeping records. Alex is a classic melancholy. "I really like budgeting. I like seeing the inflow and outflow of money. I put it in Excel. It helps me not feel stressed. Without a budget, if I saw that my bank balance was down by a thousand dollars, I would be stressed. But knowing where it went helps me."

If anything, melancholies may be too detail-oriented, striving for the perfect budget and getting frustrated if the numbers are slightly off. They can also be a bit unrealistic, setting financial goals that are beyond the reach of most mortals.

Melancholies are also good at controlling spending. Their

sacrificial nature helps them delay gratification, putting up with an old car until they have enough money saved to buy their next car with cash.

However, a perfectionist streak may cause melancholies to over-spend on certain things, especially those related to their aesthetic nature: artwork, beautiful clothing, or tickets to see a favorite band. For example, I mentioned that Jude has a great ability to live within her means (which comes from her secondary temperament of phlegmatic), so you would think that overspending is not an issue in our relation-ship. However, her primary temperament is melancholy, and she has the classic melancholy tendency toward being a perfectionist when it comes to certain things—in her case, eyeglasses. A few years into our marriage, we both agreed that she could use a new pair of glasses. Did we go to one of the national chains or a department store? No way. She insisted on going to a small boutique in Chicago's fashionable Lincoln Park neighborhood, where she picked out not one pair of pricey specs, but two! Now I know she will always have high expectations, and we'll need a healthy budget for eyeglasses. Fortunately, her phlegmatic side makes her content to keep her glasses for a long time.

Fear can make melancholies under-perform in their work, as they are hesitant to ask for much of a salary when interviewing for a new job. Their self-doubt makes them fear missing out on the job if they ask for too much. Their sense of altruism may also impact career decisions. A martyr mindset, feeling the need to suffer for their cause, may lead them to low-paid work that is aligned with their values.

Melancholy pros/cons and what to do. Your natural desire to use a budget gives you and your spouse a huge financial advantage. Your main watch-out is a tendency to succumb to fear. It can hold you back in your career as you strive for too little, and it can lead you to be overly cautious as an investor. Take encouragement from Scripture, where the most frequent command is "Do not fear." Then practice overcoming fear in low-risk settings, such as working up the nerve to ask a waiter for a better table as he walks you to a high-traffic table near the kitchen door. Getting some wins under your belt will prepare you to make scarier requests, such as asking for a raise.

Bonus Idea. Want to buy a melancholy spouse a great gift? Choose something that appeals to your mate's aesthetic sensibilities, such as tickets to a concert or play.

HOW ABOUT YOU?

Were each of you able to identify your primary and secondary temperaments? Spend some time discussing how you see your temperaments impacting your views and uses of money, and then talk about how your temperaments might complement each other in dealing with money and also how they might collide.

Remember, temperaments don't change, but they can be managed by doing some of the things discussed in this chapter.

FROM INSIGHTS TO ACTION

At this point you have learned more of the details of each other's financial lives, talked about your financial past, and gained an understanding of how your temperaments impact your views and use of money. Now it's time to put these insights into action through the daily process of managing money together. The next section will guide you through a step-by-step process for doing so successfully.

PART TWO

A TEN-STEP ACTION PLAN FOR FINANCIAL SUCCESS

CHAPTER 5

PLAN TO SUCCEED

The plans of the diligent lead to profit as surely as haste leads to poverty.

PROVERBS 21:5

Budget: A mathematical confirmation of your suspicions.

A. A. LATIMER

WHEN MARRIAGE BLOGGER DUSTIN Riechmann (www .engagedmarriage.com) asked his readers "What were some of the *biggest initial challenges* you faced in bringing your financial lives together? Financially, what do you wish you had known or done before getting married?" Cassidy responded,

> The biggest challenge my husband and I faced was finding common ground in our spending habits. In our case, that challenge came very quickly because our first baby was born a couple months before our first anniversary. She made it so our priority became setting aside our frivolous spending to make sure we could get the things our baby needed. I wish I had known in the beginning just how important a budget was. We always had an idea of what we would spend on things

<59>

each month, but it was a very relaxed idea and we didn't really track it. Even when money isn't tight, it is very important to keep a budget and track spending. I wish we had both known that before money became tight and we had to learn it the hard way. We evaluate our spending a lot. I think our budget and what we want to spend money on is our most frequent financial topic. After nearly six years of marriage, we are finally on the same page with our money the majority of the time. It's great to be at a point where we're both working toward the same goals and not having to always debate what we'll spend money on.[1]

As Cassidy discovered, one of the best marital money moves you can make is to use a budget. Why? Because the most common financial disagreement among married couples has to do with how much to spend on various items. Of couples that have money fights "often" or "sometimes," 49 percent say that spending decisions are what they fight about most often.[2]

It's no wonder that spending decisions top the list of married couples' financial fights, given that just 23 percent of couples say they work together to plan their financial lives[3] and a mere 12 percent use a detailed budget to guide their financial decisions.[4]

AN IMAGE PROBLEM

Believe me, I know that using a budget is not the most appealing idea in the world. Whenever I ask people at my financial workshops who comes to mind when they think of a budget, typical answers include the Grinch and Scrooge. One person said Darth Vader; another said the Devil. In one workshop, a newly married man said, "My mother-in-law."

Many people think of a budget as something you *go on* like a diet, as in, "We can't ask Joe and Lucy to join us for dinner at a restaurant; they're *on* a budget." They equate the use of a budget as nothing but work, a life of restrictions, or obsessive frugality. Not exactly the stuff that will get you out of bed in the morning.

But the bad rap that budgets get is underserved.

THE GOOD THAT BUDGETS CAN DO

I firmly believe that a budget or, as I prefer, a *Cash Flow Plan*, is the single most powerful personal finance tool for managing money successfully. You may have to take this on faith, but using a *Cash Flow Plan* is the ticket to financial freedom, not a life of restrictions. When you know how much you have left in your grocery budget before heading to the grocery store, you are free to spend that money. You won't drag any nagging questions into the produce aisle about how splurging on organic bananas may impact your ability to help your kids pay for college.

Using a *Cash Flow Plan* also takes some of the emotion out of financial disagreements because it gives you objective information. In fact, married couples who use a budget are less likely to have financial disagreements than those who don't use one,[5] and couples who use a detailed budget have fewer financial fights than those who use a general budget.

A budget really shines when you link its use to specific financial goals you're trying to achieve. Consider the four quadrants in the upcoming chart. If you don't have goals and don't have a plan (the lower right quadrant), you are wandering. You don't know where you want to go and have no plan for getting there. If you don't have goals but have a plan (lower left quadrant), you may be obsessing over your finances. You're keeping tabs over the details of your finances but with no ultimate purpose or destination in mind. If you have goals but no plan (upper right quadrant), you may be dreaming. You have a vision for where you'd like to go but no plan for getting there. Lastly, if you have goals and a plan (upper left quadrant), you are truly managing money. When couples use a *Cash Flow Plan* to pursue specific, agreed-upon financial goals, it's a combination that can't be beat.

Goal Quadrant

	Cash Flow Plan		No Cash Flow Plan

Goals

Managing

Dreaming

Obsessing

Wandering

No Goals

FLEXIBILITY BUILT IN

A *Cash Flow Plan* is just what it sounds like: a plan you develop with your spouse that predetermines what you will do with your income. When you decide ahead of time how much you will give and save and how much you can spend on personal items such as clothing, hair styling, groceries, vacations, and such, there's no reason to worry or fight over the thought that one of you is overspending, assuming that you're both sticking to the agreed-upon amounts.

I remember a time early in our marriage when Jude and I went clothes shopping together and I decided to buy a sweater that, at first, Jude thought was outrageously expensive. When she realized that it was within my clothing budget, even though it would require devoting my entire month's clothing allocation, she came around to the idea that it was okay. That's how a budget works. If you want to spend the full amount on one item, it's up to you.

This chapter will teach you how to set up and use a *Cash Flow Plan* and then will walk you through three systems for putting your plan into action. The rest of the chapters in this section will guide you through each of the categories on the *Cash Flow Plan*, with recommendations on how to effectively manage each category.

I chose those last words carefully. Please do not think of a budget as being about less, as in spending less in every category. Think about it as being about more, as in having more knowledge about where your money is going so that you can be more effective in choosing where it should go and so you can have more for what matters most.

If you are not married yet, both of you should set up your own budgets and get in the habit of using this powerful tool before you marry. Before your wedding day, you should also work together to draft a budget for your first year of marriage.

A BUDGET HOW-TO GUIDE

Here are the four steps for successfully setting up and using a *Cash Flow Plan*:

1. Estimate today
2. Plan for tomorrow
3. Monitor reality
4. Review and revise

1. Estimate Today
The first step in developing a *Cash Flow Plan* is to estimate your current income and expenses. Go ahead and fill in the "Now" columns on the *Monthly Cash Flow Plan*. (An example of the form is on page 64. You can download full-sized forms for free from my website at www

Monthly Cash Flow Plan

	Now	Goal		Now	Goal
Monthly Income			**Taxes**		
Salary 1 (gross)			Federal		
Salary 2 (gross)			State		
			Social Security (FICA)		
Giving			Medicare		
Faith-based			Other		
Other					
			Food		
Savings			**Clothing**		
Emergency fund					
< 5-yrs. goal _____			**Household/Personal**		
			Dry cleaning		
Debts			Gifts		
Credit card			Furniture/household items		
Credit card			Cosmetics		
Credit card			Barber/beauty		
Car/truck loan			Allowances		
Education			Education		
Other					
			Entertainment		
Investing			Restaurants/movies		
Retirement			Cable/satellite TV		
College			Vacation		
> 5-yrs. goal _____			Books/subscriptions		
			Health club/hobbies		
Housing			Pets		
Mortgage/rent					
Real estate tax			**Health**		
Insurance			Medical/dental insurance		
			Prescriptions/co-pays		
Maintenance/Utilities			HSA/FSA		
Maintenance			Disability insurance		
Electric			Life insurance		
Gas					
Water/Garbage			**Professional Services**		
Home phone/Internet			Legal/accounting		
Cell phone			Counseling		
			Child care/babysitting		
Transportation					
Gas			**Miscellaneous**		
Vehicle maintenance					
Insurance			**Total Monthly Income**		
Bus/train/parking/tolls			**Total Monthly Outgo**		
License/fees			**Income Minus Outgo**		

.MattAbout Money.com/resources.) Some of the categories will be easy to complete. You know your fixed expenses, such as your rent or mortgage payment and various insurance bills. However, you might not know how much you spend each month on entertainment or clothing. That's okay. For now, just take an educated guess.

For expenses or bills that occur less often than monthly, such as a semiannual insurance premium or a yearly vacation, take the annual amount you spend, divide by twelve, and enter that amount. Be sure to include at least fifty dollars for miscellaneous because there are always expenses that don't fit neatly into one of the preplanned categories.

In the bottom right corner of the form, subtract your total estimated monthly outgo from your total estimated monthly income.

2. Plan for Tomorrow

Next, fill in the "Goal" columns. I don't have an opinion as to what brand of car you should drive or where you should go on vacation, but I do have recommendations about the best way to prioritize your use of money, which is reflected in the order in which the categories appear on the *Monthly Cash Flow Plan*. In Appendix A, you will find detailed recommended-spending plans for one- and two-person households. Establishing these spending priorities and following the percentage recommendations will help you build a solid financial foundation from which you can pursue your unique financial goals.

3. Monitor Reality

The next step is to monitor your cash flow in one of three ways: the envelope system, a paper-and-pencil system, or an electronic system. As you read the following descriptions, see which one best suits you.

The envelope system. (Best for people who prefer to use cash whenever possible but also pay some bills online. Also a good system for those who *do not* have much money in reserve.)

Each time you get paid, fill envelopes with the amount of cash you have budgeted for specific spending categories until the next time you are paid. For instance, if you get paid once a month and have $400 budgeted for groceries, each time you get paid put $400 in cash into an envelope labeled "Groceries." If you get paid twice a month, put $200 in the envelope each time you receive a paycheck. If you get paid every two weeks (26 times per year), put $185 in your "Groceries" envelope ($400 per month multiplied by 12 = $4,800 for the year, divided by 26 = $185). When you go grocery shopping, take that envelope with you, pay for your groceries with the money in the envelope, and put the change back in the envelope.

Every time you spend money out of one of the envelopes, write down on the outside of the envelope how much you spent, the date, where you spent it, and what it was for. This record will come in handy at the end of each month. You'll be able to analyze where you spent your money and see if you'd like to make any changes next month.

You won't want to use an envelope for every spending category. For example, you probably have an automatic mortgage payment taken out of your checking account each month. Same thing for utilities, such as gas and electricity. But envelopes work well for categories like home maintenance, gasoline, vehicle maintenance, bus/train/parking/tolls, food, clothing, dry cleaning, gifts, entertainment, and miscellaneous. If you and your spouse have separate clothing allocations, create a "His Clothing" envelope and a "Her Clothing" envelope.

When you're out of money in a certain envelope, you're done spending in that category until your next payday. If there's any money left over at the end of a period in one or more of the envelopes, keep the money in the envelope so you have more to spend over the next period. This is especially important for categories like vehicle and home maintenance. Some months you will spend little in these areas, but other months you will have to spend a lot, so you will be glad the money has been accumulating.

Paper-and-pencil system. (Best for people who use a combination of cash, debit/credit cards, and online bill pay and have some money in reserve.)

Track your spending by keeping receipts or by writing down how much you spend during the day and then entering that information on the *Monthly Cash Flow Tracker* at the end of each day. There's an example of this form on page 68; make copies of it, as you will use one form for each month. Also, you can download full-sized copies from my website.

Across the top of the *Monthly Cash Flow Tracker*, in the "Goals" row, enter your income and expense goals from the *Monthly Cash Flow Plan*. The reason there are not enough rows for every day of the month is because you aren't likely to spend money in every category every day; the rows underneath "Goals" are not meant to represent each day of the month. The column underneath "Goals" is for whatever notes you may want to add. Perhaps you'd like a reminder that a gift expense was for Uncle Stan or that an entertainment expense was for a movie.

The numbers across the bottom of the form represent the days of the month. This can help you remember to write down your daily expenses. People who are new to the budgeting process sometimes forget to write down their spending for a day or two. As they lose track of their spending, they become frustrated and give up. Crossing off today's date at the bottom of the form after entering the day's spending let's you know you've recorded all of your expenses for the day.

At the end of the month, total up each category and then indicate how much over or under your actual spending was compared to the goal. Look at the previous month's *Cash Flow Tracker* to see how much over or under you were up to that point in the year, and enter that on this month's form. Then total up how much over or under you are for the year.

An electronic system. There are three different electronic systems.

- *Excel spreadsheet.* (Best for people who like the layout of the paper-and-pencil system but prefer to use an electronic tool.)
  On my website (www.MattAboutMoney.com/resources) you'll find downloadable Excel spreadsheets formatted just like the paper-and-pencil *Monthly Cash Flow Plan* and *Monthly*

Monthly Cash Flow Tracker

Month _____

	Income	Giving	Saving/ Investing	Debts	Housing		Transp.	Income Taxes	Food	Clothing	Household/Personal			Ent.	Health	Prof. Svcs.	Misc.
					Mort./Rent, Real Estate Tax, Ins.	Home Maint./ Utilities					Gifts	Beauty/ Barber	All Other				
(1) Goals																	
1																	
2																	
3																	
4																	
5																	
6																	
7																	
8																	
9																	
10																	
11																	
12																	
13																	
14																	
15																	
16																	
17																	
18																	
19																	
20																	
21																	
22																	
23																	
24																	
25																	
26																	
27																	
28																	
29																	
30																	
31																	
(2) Total																	
(3) Over/Under																	
(4) Last Mo. YTD																	
(5) Total YTD																	

(1) Enter your goals for each category from your *Monthly Cash Flow Plan.* Then record your daily spending, crossing off the day of the month at the bottom of this page as a reminder that you have recorded the day's spending. Use the space in the "Goals" column to add any notes that will help you remember certain expenses.

(2) Total each category at the end of the month.

(3) Record how much you are over or under the monthly goal for the category.

(4) Enter last month's total year-to-date figures for each category.

(5) Create a new year-to-date total.

Cash Flow Tracker. This can simplify some aspects of the paper-and-pencil system by totaling your columns automatically.

- *Budget software.* (Best for people who are computer savvy and like detail in their budgets.)

  Quicken is the main game in town. (This product is strongest for PC users; the Mac version does not offer as many features.) After buying the software, load it onto a computer via a disc or download the program online. Quicken can download your checking, savings, and credit card transactions through an online connection with your bank and credit card companies. It can also download the latest information from your investment accounts. Two other software programs that have gotten especially good reviews are Mvelopes (www.mvelopes .com) and You Need a Budget (www.youneedabudget.com).

  One downside to budget software is the cost. To overcome this issue, let's look at the third category of electronic tools.

- *Online tools.* (Best for people who are comfortable doing online banking, prefer to have their budget available online, and don't need a ton of detail.)

  These are the newest players in the electronic budgeting space. The first step in using an online budget tool is the most unnerving for the uninitiated: You must enter your bank and credit card account numbers and passwords. The leading providers know that people's number one concern is security, so they go to the nth degree in making sure their systems are secure. Still, if you're not comfortable with this, use one of the other systems.

  Once you are set up to allow the service to access your records, it will download your latest transactions automatically. It can also be set up to automatically categorize certain transactions for you. For example, if you do most of your grocery shopping at Safeway, you can instruct the system to categorize all Safeway transactions as groceries. You can also go in and manually make adjustments, such as when you get cash back or pick up a prescription.

The players in this category include Mint (www.mint .com), moneyStrands (https://money.strands.com/), and others. See my website for my latest reviews and recommendations.

If you are new to budgeting, I recommend that you use a manual system like the envelope system or the paper-and-pencil system for at least the first year. They will give you more of a hands-on feel for the budgeting process. Once you get comfortable with budgeting, you could switch to an electronic system.

4. Review and Revise

Finally, look at your actual cash flow compared to your plan. Do this evaluation at the end of every month. You might do your monthly reviews during a money date. You don't have to go out to a fancy restaurant, but sometimes getting out of the house helps provide more objectivity in reviewing how you're doing compared with your plan.

If you are way off in a certain category, one of two things is probably true. First, you weren't proactive enough in managing to the number. Perhaps you knew the monthly target for a certain category but never checked to see how much of the budget was left until the end of the month, and by that time you had overspent the category. You'll need to spend less in the months ahead to catch up, and you'll need to get in the habit of checking to see how you're doing before spending more in a category.

Second, your budget target in one or more categories was unrealistic. Maybe you need to plan to spend more on groceries than you thought, which will mean you'll have to plan to spend less for a different category.

Now for some of the most common budget questions I get in workshops and through my blog.

COMMON BUDGETING QUESTIONS

How Do We Manage an Irregular Income?

This is a frequent question among people who are in sales and depend on commissions for a significant portion of their income. One of the mistakes salespeople often make is being overconfident, especially after a good month. They come to see their income from that month as the amount they will make every month. It's far better to be conservative.

If you've had your variable-income job for several years, look back at how much you made during most months and set your budget on that amount. I'd rather have you be surprised by earning more than you anticipated than the other way around. During those good months, pad your emergency fund with the extra money so it's there for you during the down months.

If you are self-employed, set up a separate business checking account and deposit all of your revenue there. Then pay yourself a fixed salary out of that account.

Does Every Spending Decision Have to Be Made Together?

It'll be good for your marriage to have "his" and "hers" budget categories. As I said before, Jude and I do that for clothing. Other couples also set up separate "fun money" allocations, which can be used for lunches with friends or hobbies. You decide what the money is for. The important thing is to each have some money you can spend as you want. You don't need permission from your spouse before spending this money; you just need to stick to the budgeted amount every month.

Who Should Manage the Budget?

Most couples still divvy up money-related tasks along traditional lines. Men typically take responsibility for investments, retirement planning, and buying insurance. Women take care of the day-to-day spending, budgeting, and bill paying.[6]

But there's no reason why it has to be that way. Usually, one spouse will more naturally gravitate toward taking on certain responsibilities, such as keeping the budget up to date. This person might also run the monthly reports. However, both of you need to agree on your spending targets, keep receipts, take responsibility not to overspend, and participate in the monthly review, even if one of you has a primary temperament of sanguine!

Working together on your *Cash Flow Plan* will help you both become better money managers, which will strengthen your marriage. Researcher Jeffrey Dew of Utah State University has found that when one spouse feels that the other does not handle money well, they are less happy in their marriage. In fact, the feeling that one's spouse handles money foolishly increases the likelihood of divorce by 45 percent among both men and women.[7]

Early in their marriage, Jessica and Alex ran into a problem with their budget. "I buy the groceries," Jessica explained, "but Alex sets the budget for groceries. One time in the middle of a month, we had used up our entire grocery budget." Mostly, it was a communication issue. Jessica needed more information about where they stood with the grocery budget throughout the month.

She says, "It was hard for me to understand how we had run out of grocery money. It hit me for the first time that my paycheck was under Alex's watch and I didn't have a complete picture of where it was really going. He saw the credit card bills; I didn't. For the first couple of months, we just talked in general terms. He would tell me, 'We made the budget.' Now we talk in more detail."

How Do We Keep from Overspending with Our Credit Cards?

For many years, I waited until we paid our credit card bills before categorizing all the spending we did on those cards over the previous month. That's the wrong way to track your use of credit cards. The right way is to treat your credit cards the same way you treat cash or checks: Enter the spending as you go.

This is easy to do if you are downloading credit card transactions with budget software like Quicken or using an online budget tool like Mint. Your credit card transactions will show up within a couple of days of the spending. If you track your spending with a paper-and-pencil tool like the *Cash Flow Plan* or manually enter transactions into an Excel spreadsheet, record your credit card purchases as you make them. When you buy a shirt with a credit card, it counts against your clothing budget now, not when you pay your credit card bill. Keeping track of your credit card spending as you go will prevent you from being surprised when you get your credit card statement at the end of the month.

NEW HABITS TAKE TIME

I hope this chapter has motivated you to get in the habit of using a budget. Even if the idea still doesn't make your heart jump for joy, give it a go. I am confident that once you get used to it, you'll find that a budget is extremely helpful for managing money successfully and as a team.

In the next chapter, we'll explore some issues that are important to your economic engine, better known as your income.

TAKE ACTION

What to Do
Decide which cash flow tracking system you will use: the envelope system, a paper-and-pencil system, an electronic spreadsheet, budget software, or an online budget tool.

What to Discuss
- Do you like or dislike the idea of using a *Cash Flow Plan*? Why?
- What hesitations do you have about using a *Cash Flow Plan*?
- What benefits do you think could come from it?

- Which one of you is best suited to handle the data entry?
- In what ways do you see your temperaments impacting your attitudes about using a *Cash Flow Plan*?

CHAPTER 6

WORK WISELY

Whatever you do, work at it with all your heart, as working for the Lord, not for men.

COLOSSIANS 3:23

Work while you have the light. You are responsible for the talent that has been entrusted to you.

HENRI-FREDERIC AMIEL

DO YOU REMEMBER THE fable "The Goose That Laid the Golden Eggs"? A couple owned an amazing goose that produced a golden egg every day. But soon one golden egg a day wasn't enough; they wanted more. So, assuming that the inside of the bird must be made out of gold, they cut it open only to discover nothing but typical goose innards. That, of course, marked the end of their daily dose of gold.

Your income-producing abilities are like that goose. Take care of those abilities, and they will take care of you and your family.

WORK DILIGENTLY

In this day and age, jobs come and go all too easily. While there's no such thing as guaranteed employment, there is something close to

<75>

guaranteed employability. That comes from putting into practice the classic counsel from God's Word found at the beginning of this chapter.

How would you work if you truly saw God as your boss? Would you come to work early? Would you put in the maximum amount of effort? You bet you would. You would do all you could to be great at your job. When we have the attitude that God is our boss, it doesn't matter what our job is or whether we think it is something we'll be doing only temporarily; we do it to the best of our ability. This was true of a guy I once knew who fell on hard times. Everything about this guy said he came from wealth. His wardrobe, his way of speaking, his manners. Even though he came from money, he was out of money, so he started driving a cab. He decided he would be the most amazing cab driver his town had ever seen. He went to people's front doors and carried their luggage to the cab. He held the door for them. He was endlessly courteous. He built a list of regular customers, and he made great money in tips.

Like this taxi driver, bring your best to whatever you do, for God and for your family. "If anyone does not provide for his relatives, and especially for his immediate family, he has denied the faith and is worse than an unbeliever" (1 Timothy 5:8).

LEARN CONTINUOUSLY

Besides being diligent in your work, doing your best also means staying on the leading edge of ideas and skills in your field. Most large employers offer some form of tuition reimbursement, and yet just 10 percent of eligible employees take advantage of that benefit.[1] That's valuable money being left on the table. Is tuition assistance available to you? If so, take advantage of that benefit. Find out what types of courses would be covered and go to school. You'll learn more about your field while making important contacts among your classmates and teachers. If you don't have kids yet, now is the ideal time to pick up a night class. If you are not eligible for tuition reimbursement, you can take other steps. Just reading the latest books and subscribing to the blogs of the leading thinkers in your field will give you an advantage over others.

FIND A GREAT COACH

Very often, successful people are more than willing to mentor younger people in their field. Who do you know who is a leader in your line of work? It might be someone at your company, someone who works for another company, a family friend, or someone you know from church. Ask if the person wouldn't mind spending some time with you to share how he or she got to this point and to teach you new aspects of your profession.

BUILD A NETWORK

One of the harshest lessons from the recent recession was just how fragile a job can be. Many thousands of people lost their jobs, and the average unemployed person stayed out of work for more than six months. A related lesson is the importance of continuous networking.

Online networking. If you don't use LinkedIn (www.linkedin .com), set up an account, build your profile, and start building your network by inviting colleagues, people you do business with, former coworkers, and former classmates to be part of your network. If you need a contact at a company, you can search for that company and if any of your contacts are connected with someone there, you'll be able to see that connection. You can then ask your contact to make an introduction.

Offline networking. Networking has gotten something of a bad name in recent years because it came to be seen as self-serving. People were encouraged to join organizations or go to events for the sole purpose of making connections. Today, networking events are more clearly promoted as such. If you're looking for work, there's nothing wrong with taking part in these events. Everyone knows why everyone else is there. When you attend networking events, because you may be meeting a lot of people in a short amount of time, focus on collecting other people's business cards more than handing out your own. That enables you to control the follow-up process rather than waiting and hoping someone will contact you. Jot a reminder of what you talked about on the back of each person's card and send personalized follow-up notes.

While overt networking events can be helpful to your career, you will find it more enjoyable and more effective to join clubs or other organizations you are genuinely interested in. You're more likely to make good contacts through your involvement in activities you care about than by joining groups for the sole purpose of networking.

Keep in mind that every time you meet someone new, you may be able to help that person, and vice versa. So we could all use a reminder of some foundational social graces, such as being more interested in others than you are in yourself. Most people enjoy talking with people who ask good questions and take a genuine interest in others.

SET YOUR PRIORITIES

With a *Cash Flow Plan* in hand and income flowing into your lives, it's time to prioritize your use of that income. There are only a handful of options for what you can do with your income. You can spend it, save it, invest it, pay down debt with it, or give it away. The order you choose will make all the difference in your financial success and satisfaction. In the next chapter, we will look at the first financial priority taught in the Bible, which is generosity.

TAKE ACTION

What to Do

Fill in the "Income" section in the "Goal" column of the *Cash Flow Plan* on page 64. In most cases, your income goal will be the same as your current income, so just enter the same number in both columns. The only exception is if you expect some change in your income within the next month. Remember, if you're not married yet, both of you should complete a *Cash Flow Plan*. Then fill out a third *Cash Flow Plan* as a draft of your first year's budget as husband and wife.

What to Discuss

- If you could eavesdrop on your coworkers, what do you think you'd hear them saying about your work habits? Would that motivate you to make any changes?

- Does your employer offer tuition reimbursement? If so, have you utilized that benefit? If not, find out what types of classes qualify for reimbursement and report back to each other. What type of class or workshop would be helpful to your career?

- What books have you read about your field in the last year? Who are the leading thinkers in your industry? How are you keeping up with them? What, if any, blogs do you read?

- Who would make for a great mentor? Are you willing to ask him or her to meet with you on a regular basis? Why or why not?

- What have you done to build a network of great contacts? What more could you do?

CHAPTER 7

GIVE SOME AWAY

It is more blessed to give than to receive.

JESUS (ACTS 20:35)

I have found that among its other benefits, giving liberates the soul of the giver.

MAYA ANGELOU

IT IS COMPLETELY APPROPRIATE to have some fun with money, go on nice vacations, purchase a comfortable home, eat out, and enjoy the many other things money can buy, assuming you're not going into debt in the process. However, the greatest satisfaction you will experience in your use of money will come from the investments you make in God's work. With a shared vision for using your marriage to impact the world, making such investments will bring you closer together and give you joy.

I made generosity the first outgo category on the *Cash Flow Plan* (see page 64) because God teaches us to make generosity our highest financial priority: "Honor the LORD with your wealth and with the firstfruits of all your produce" (Proverbs 3:9, ESV). *Firstfruits* means the first portion.

It isn't that God needs our money. He makes that abundantly clear

<81>

in Psalm 50:12: "If I were hungry I would not tell you, for the world is mine, and all that is in it." In other words, God created and owns everything. He can make anything happen anytime. He isn't looking for a bailout or a handout. Still, he teaches us to be generous. Here's why.

WHY GIVE?

Designed to Be Generous

God is infinitely generous. He gave us our lives and the people in our lives. He gave us his Son. Because we were made in his image (see Genesis 1:27), generosity is a central part of who we are. It's woven into the fabric of our souls. When we are generous, we live in concert with our design, so it should come as no surprise that modern-day researchers studying the causes of human happiness have found that generous people are happier than those who are not generous.[1]

A Tangible Reminder of Our Highest Priority

The main purpose of our lives is this: "Love the Lord your God with all your heart and with all your soul and with all your mind" (Matthew 22:37). What's the main roadblock to living out that priority? Money. Jesus said, "No one can serve two masters. Either he will hate the one and love the other, or he will be devoted to the one and despise the other. You cannot serve both God and Money" (Matthew 6:24). Jesus could have talked about the impossibility of serving God and our spouse, or our vocation, or our hobbies, or any number of other things. It's true we are not to put any of those priorities above our relationship with Christ, but God highlighted money because he knew it would be his chief rival for our hearts.

When we give money to further God's work, we tangibly remind ourselves that he is our highest priority. What is God's work in the world? You'll find the answer in the next reason why God teaches us to make generosity our highest financial priority.

Amazing Returns on Investment

When we invest our generosity dollars in God's purposes, the return on our investment is always positive. Here are three such purposes.

1. Spreading the gospel. Jesus said, "Go and make disciples of all nations, baptizing them in the name of the Father and of the Son and of the Holy Spirit, and teaching them to obey everything I have commanded you" (Matthew 28:19-20). When we receive our monthly brokerage account statements, some months our investment returns are up and other months they're down, but when we receive the monthly newsletters of missionary friends we support, the results are always up. Those newsletters are filled with stories of people who placed their faith in Christ as a result, at least in part, of the ministries in which we have invested.

2. Alleviating the suffering of the poor. God's heart for the poor is written throughout the pages of Scripture. The Bible says, "He who is kind to the poor lends to the LORD, and he will reward him for what he has done" (Proverbs 19:17).

Earthquakes, hurricanes, plane crashes, and other disasters make news headlines around the world, as they should. However, there is a much larger disaster that occurs every day. According to the United Nations, an estimated 24,000 children die each day due to poverty, hunger, easily preventable diseases, illnesses, and other related causes.[2] When we invest in the work of ministries that are serving the poor, helping to provide food, clean water, job training, medical care, and more, we are helping to literally save people's lives.

3. Supporting teachers of God's Word. There is no more important training we receive than instruction in God's Word. We are called to help fund the work of those who do such teaching. The apostle Paul said, "Anyone who receives instruction in the word must share all good things with his instructor" (Galatians 6:6).

So think about that. By investing in God's purposes, we can actually help alter people's eternities, save people's lives, and further the teaching of God's Word. Those are amazing returns on investment.

The Personal Blessings of Generosity

Here's a final reason to make generosity our highest financial priority: The Bible promises that we will be blessed by living with a spirit of generosity. At the beginning of this chapter, we read Proverbs 3:9: "Honor the LORD with your wealth, with the firstfruits of all your crops." Verse 10 adds, "Then your barns will be filled to overflowing, and your vats will brim over with new wine."

Numerous other verses in the Old and New Testaments make the same point. Consider:

One man gives freely, yet gains even more;
    another withholds unduly, but comes to poverty.
A generous man will prosper;
    he who refreshes others will himself be refreshed. (Proverbs 11:24-25)

"Bring the whole tithe into the storehouse, that there may be food in my house. Test me in this," says the LORD Almighty, "and see if I will not throw open the floodgates of heaven and pour out so much blessing that you will not have room enough for it." (Malachi 3:10; this is the only place in the Bible where God says to test him)

Give, and it will be given to you. A good measure, pressed down, shaken together and running over, will be poured into your lap. For with the measure you use, it will be measured to you. (Luke 6:38)

Remember this: Whoever sows sparingly will also reap sparingly, and whoever sows generously will also reap generously. (2 Corinthians 9:6)

It has become a bit trickier to teach about this aspect of generosity due to the spread of what's known as the prosperity gospel, which teaches a "Give to get" approach to generosity. Giving primarily out of a motivation to receive something back is surely an affront to God. As the apostle Paul asked, "Who has ever given to God, that God should repay him?" (Romans 11:35). God is the giver; we are the recipients of all he has generously given to us.

Still, there is an unmistakable promise seen throughout the pages of Scripture that blessings flow from generosity motivated by a grateful heart. Some people trace material blessings to their generosity. Others have experienced a closer relationship with God. In one form or another, blessings come from our generosity. It's how things work in God's economy.

Now that we've looked at *why* we should give, let's look at *how much* to give and *where* to give.

HOW MUCH TO GIVE

As a starting point, give away 10 percent of your gross income, which is what the Bible refers to as a tithe. The tithe was part of the Old Testament law (see Leviticus 27:30), but it even transcended the law, with the first example of someone giving 10 percent going all the way back to the first book of the Bible (see Genesis 14:20). In the New Testament, it is clear that 10 percent is not the intended stopping point. We read of Zacchaeus, who gave away half of what he owned (see Luke 19:1-10), and about the poor widow who gave all that she had (see Luke 21:1-4).

The Bible teaches that the main reason God enables us to prosper is so that we will grow in generosity: "You will be made rich in every way so that you can be generous on every occasion" (2 Corinthians 9:11).

WHERE TO GIVE

Look for trustworthy places to invest in the three priorities I mentioned earlier: bringing the gospel to those who don't know God, helping the poor, and supporting teachers of God's Word. Some pastors teach that all of a person's tithe should go to the church. They encourage supporting other Christian ministries but only with money above and beyond the tithe. If you are part of such a church, I encourage you to follow your pastor's teaching.

In our family, a majority of our faith-based giving goes to our church because it's a one-stop shop for those three priorities. It helps reach the lost by supporting several missionaries and by preaching the gospel to those who come to our church for the first time. It also helps meet the needs of the poor in our community and in other parts of the world, and it is where we learn more of God's Word. However, we also give to other kingdom-centered organizations God has put on our hearts.

....

What About Museums and Other Nonprofits?

There are many great causes in the world, and I encourage you to support the nonprofits whose work you care about. However, if you are a Christian, the first priority for your generosity dollars is to support God's work in the world. Only these investments have the potential to generate eternity-shaping returns. That's why I recommended in chapter 2 that you distinguish between the faith-based organizations you support and all others.

....

HOW A BUDGET HELPS

Jessica and Alex, who got married right out of college, agreed before getting married that they would tithe. But Alex candidly acknowledges it was a struggle to follow through. "I was getting my first salary, which wasn't a lot, but it was a lot more than I made when I was in school, so it seemed like a lot of money to give away."

The use of a budget helped. Once they plugged in all the numbers, covering their living expenses, allocating some fun money for each of them, and designating 10 percent of their income for giving, they were happily surprised to discover that they had a surplus of 3 percent.

Jessica said, "The budget was the key. We never would have known we would have had extra. We felt as though we were poor, and we assumed it wouldn't work. If we didn't have a budget to show us that we were fine, giving 10 percent would have been tough."

HOW CAN WE GIVE WHEN WE'RE IN DEBT?

Debt is one of the primary roadblocks to all of the good things money can do, including the ability to live generously. As we'll discuss in chapter 9, the best way to speed up the process of getting out of debt is to pay more than the minimum due each month. The money you are giving away each month can look like an easy source of those additional funds. However, before tapping that money, here are three recommendations.

1. Pray for discernment. God knows your situation, so ask him what you should do. I know people who have taken this step who have sensed God telling them to give at least at the 10 percent level, even though it would take them longer to get out of debt. So that's what they did, trusting that God had a purpose in mind that could be accomplished only through an extended time of debt repayment.

2. Rethink other budget categories first. Because of the high value God places on generosity, before deciding to give less than a tithe, consider other ways to free up money for accelerated debt repayment, even crazy-sounding ways. How about cutting out cable TV while getting out of debt or even going without an Internet connection at home? How about going from a two-car family to a one-car family? How about going on a temporary entertainment-spending fast, seeking out all of the free things to do for fun in your community?

3. Always give a choice gift. If you sense God's freedom to give less than a tithe for a season, at very least keep in mind the biblical standard of a firstfruits gift. That's a first priority, or a choice gift. Think back to the story of Cain and Abel, Adam and Eve's sons (see Genesis 4:3-5). When they both brought offerings to the Lord, Cain brought "some of the fruits of the soil," which scholars have explained means that he gave a portion of his crops but not the best portion. By contrast, Abel brought "fat portions from some of the firstborn of his flock." In other words, he gave a choice gift. "The LORD looked with favor on Abel and his offering, but on Cain and his offering he did not look with favor" (verses 4-5).

THE GREAT FINANCIAL PARADOX

Our culture advises, "Pay yourself first." It makes intuitive sense, doesn't it? If we are to experience financial success, our first financial priority must be to set aside a portion of all that we earn for savings or investing. Yet money is a struggle for so many people. God's solution is the counterintuitive teaching, "Pay your purpose first." Because the overarching purpose of our lives is to love God, the most tangible way we can fulfill that purpose financially is to make the support of His work in the world our highest financial priority. Go ahead and put such teaching to the test. You'll soon discover the blessings that flow from living the generous life you were designed to live.

Saving a portion of all that we earn is our second financial priority.

TAKE ACTION

What to Do
Fill in the "Goal" column in the "Generosity" section of the *Cash Flow Plan* on page 64. As you read this chapter, did you feel motivated to increase the amount you are giving? Even if you have no idea how you will come up with the money, set a goal in faith.

What to Discuss
• What is your response to this chapter? Will generosity be your first financial priority in your marriage?

- What percentage of your household income will you devote to supporting God's work?
- What roadblocks hold you back in this area? Are they financial roadblocks, like debt, or emotional roadblocks, like fear?
- Is your church a one-stop shop for the three kingdom priorities highlighted in this chapter: spreading the gospel, helping the poor, and supporting teachers of God's Word? Do you know how your church supports the work of evangelism and helping the poor? If not, make a call and find out.
- What blessings have you experienced through generosity?

CHAPTER 8

PUT SOME AWAY

In the house of the wise are stores of choice food and oil, but a foolish man devours all he has.

PROVERBS 21:20

I have enough money to last me the rest of my life, unless I buy something.

JACKIE MASON

ONE OF THE SUREST ways to experience financial stress is to go through life without a financial safety net, better known as an emergency fund. Not long ago I worked with the market research firm Synovate to conduct a national survey, asking a representative sample of the population how much financial stress they were experiencing. I also asked whether they pay their credit card balances in full each month, whether they use a household budget, and how much money they have set aside for emergencies. All three habits are important. However, financial stress was most closely correlated with how much money people had in reserve. Those who had no emergency fund or considered their credit cards or a home equity line of credit to be their emergency fund were the most stressed. Those who were the least stressed had six

<91>

or more months' worth of living expenses set aside.[1]

In this chapter, we'll look at three types of savings: an emergency fund, savings for periodic bills and expenses, and savings for purchases to be made within the next five years.

AN EMERGENCY FUND

One of the few certainties in life is that things will go wrong. While everyone should plan to spend some money for out-of-pocket medical expenses as well as home and vehicle maintenance, if your expenses in these areas exceed your planned spending, that can constitute an emergency. That's what an emergency fund is for. The worst financial emergency you could experience is the loss of your income, whether through unemployment, illness, or injury. Having money in reserve is an essential key to surviving these emergencies without having to take on debt.

I used to think three to six months' worth of savings constituted a sufficient emergency fund, but during the most recent recession, I saw with fresh eyes just how bad things could get. Unemployment was high and people who lost their jobs were remaining out of work for an average of more than six months. That's why the new normal for an emergency fund is a minimum of six months' worth of living expenses.

To figure out how much that is for you, go through the *Cash Flow Plan* (see page 64) and total up all of the essential expenses you would have if you lost your income tomorrow. Vacations and entertainment are not essentials, but your mortgage, utilities, insurance, groceries, and other items are. Total up one month's worth of such expenses and then multiply that figure by six; this is your emergency fund goal.

If you do not have a sufficient emergency fund but are putting money into a retirement plan, in most cases I recommend that you stop contributing to the retirement plan until you have six month's worth of living expenses in savings. The only exception is if your employer matches some of your retirement plan contributions. That's such a good deal I'd hate for you to miss out. If you can aggressively build your emergency fund and continue contributing to your retirement plan at the level that earns you the full match, that would be ideal. If you can't do both, focus on your emergency fund until it could cover six months' worth of living expenses.

The only situation in which I recommend having less than six months' worth of expenses in savings is if you have debt other than a reasonable mortgage (I'll explain what I mean by "reasonable" later), such as credit card balances you carry from month to month, a vehicle loan, a student loan, or other debts. If that's you, build an emergency fund of one month's worth of living expenses, then focus on getting out of debt (the subject of chapter 9), and then build your emergency fund up to the full six months' worth of living expenses.

Once you have this base of savings in place, you can save and invest for other goals, but if you ever need to tap into this savings, stop other forms of savings or investing until it is built back up again.

Some good choices about where to put emergency fund money include a bank (traditional or online) or credit union savings or money market account and a money market fund. Online banks often pay higher interest rates than traditional banks while typically carrying the same FDIC insurance.

Money market funds are different than money market accounts. Money market funds are mutual funds, which carry slightly more risk than a money market account. While such funds are conservative and typically safe, they are not guaranteed against loss. Most mutual fund companies are insured by the Securities Investor Protection Corporation (SIPC), which protects you against loss should the company fail or commit fraud. However, it does not insure you against investment loss. While it is extremely rare for a money market fund to lose value, there have been a few cases where that has happened.

Money market funds often pay higher interest than what banks pay on savings and money market accounts, but not always. When choosing where to keep your emergency fund money, compare interest rates being offered by banks and credit unions with the rates on money market mutual funds, and then weigh the small risk of putting money into a money market mutual fund versus the safety of a bank or credit union.

SAVINGS FOR PERIODIC BILLS AND EXPENSES

This type of savings is for anything you spend money on during the year but not necessarily every month. Examples include: home and vehicle maintenance; any insurance premiums you pay quarterly, semiannually, or annually; property taxes (if you pay them separately from your mortgage); gifts; and vacations. If you haven't planned ahead, such bills or expenses can be real budget busters when they need to be paid.

In order to determine how much you should save each month, take the annual total of all such expenses, divide by twelve, and set up an automatic transfer of that amount into a separate savings account each month. Don't mingle this savings account with your emergency fund. Keep it in a separate account. When a periodic bill comes due, transfer the money to your checking account and make the payment. Or, with some savings accounts, you can pay bills directly.

Jude and I use this type of savings account for our annual life insurance premiums, semiannual vehicle insurance premium, property taxes, and vacations. We have budgeted amounts for home and vehicle maintenance and gifts, but we let unspent portions of our monthly allotments for those categories build up in our checking account. We find that we spend on those categories often enough that it makes more sense to keep such funds in our checking account. However, if you spend a lot on Christmas gifts, you may find it helpful to separate out your Christmas gift budget from a gift budget for all other occasions and transfer one-twelfth of your annual Christmas gift budget into this savings account each month.

SAVINGS FOR PURCHASES TO BE MADE WITHIN THE NEXT FIVE YEARS

This type of savings is for big-ticket expenditures you anticipate having to make, such as replacing a car or the roof of your house. Keep this money in a bank or credit union savings account, a money market account, a money market mutual fund, or a certificate of deposit (CD), but be sure to keep it separate from your emergency fund and the savings account you maintain for periodic bills and expenses.

Take Off the Shackles

Remember, the only exception to the guideline of keeping six months' worth of living expenses in an emergency fund is if you have debt other than a reasonable mortgage. If that's your situation, get one month's worth of living expenses in your emergency fund and then follow the four-step process for freeing yourself from the bondage of debt taught in the next chapter.

TAKE ACTION

What to Do

Fill in the "Goal" column for the "Emergency fund" line in the "Savings" section of the *Cash Flow Plan* on page 64. Estimate how much it would cost to cover your essential expenses for one month and then multiply that figure by six. If you do not have six months' worth of essential living expenses in savings, set a goal for a monthly amount you could begin putting into savings, and then set up an automatic transfer from checking into savings each month.

Savings for periodic bills and expenses doesn't go in the "Savings" section. Instead, as you complete the rest of the *Cash Flow Plan*, put a check mark next to any bill or expense that you pay at some point in the year but not necessarily every month.

Then determine which ones you will save for in a separate savings account. Add up the total annual cost of all such items, divide by twelve, and set up an automatic monthly transfer of that amount into this account.

If your emergency fund is fully funded, consider what you may need or want to buy within the next five years and write those items on the "< 5-yrs. goal" line of the *Cash Flow Plan*. Set a goal for a monthly amount you could begin setting aside for such a goal and put that amount on automatic transfer from checking into another separate savings account.

What to Discuss

- How much money will you keep in an emergency fund?
- How many months' worth of essential living expenses will you likely have in savings at the start of your marriage? Where will you keep your emergency fund?
- Do you need to stop putting so much into your retirement plans for a little while in order to focus on building an adequate emergency fund?
- How do you feel about maintaining a separate savings account for periodic bills and expenses? If you plan to put this idea into practice, what types of expenses and bills will you save for with this account? Where will you keep this account?
- Are there any big-ticket items you'd like to buy within the next five years that you should be saving for? How soon are you likely to need to replace a car, for example?

CHAPTER 9

RUTHLESSLY AVOID DEBT

The rich rule over the poor, and the borrower is servant to the lender.

PROVERBS 22:7

Debt — noun. An ingenious substitute for the chain and whip of the slave driver.

AMBROSE BIERCE, THE DEVIL'S DICTIONARY

IT TOOK ONLY A few dates for Scott to fall in love with Karen. Even though she hinted about having "a credit card situation," he didn't think much of it. Judging from her apartment, he figured she was successful. He says, "Every inch was decorated. It all looked very put together. I figured when I met her parents, they would be millionaires."

About six months into the relationship, after a few more mentions of her "credit card situation," he finally asked her how bad it was. It was $50,000 bad.

Several years before meeting Scott, Karen had been through the devastating breakup of a relationship she thought was headed toward

<97>

marriage. "I decided that if I'm not getting married, I'm going to have a nice place to live. I can still see myself standing at the counter of the furniture store buying a couch for $1,000 with a credit card and feeling very unrepentant. Then spending $20 or $30 seemed like no big deal. Within six months, I had completely redecorated my apartment."

It didn't help that Karen's freelance work made her income inconsistent. First one credit card was maxed out, then another, until she had four cards charged to their limits. "I remember going to the grocery store hoping I had enough wiggle room to buy groceries."

Telling Scott about the full extent of her financial problems marked the beginning of her turnaround. "He was incredibly supportive. I remember him sitting on the couch, and I was just bawling and he was just holding me. He was so encouraging. He said, 'I'm not the guy who can rescue you, but I can walk through this with you.'"

Scott remembers it this way: "My honest reaction was, 'Boy, that's a bummer.' Scott once had $29,000 of credit card debt and spent more than three years paying it all off. "I knew I didn't want to do that again." But it was too late. He had already fallen in love with Karen.

Karen developed a budget, cut up her credit cards, accepted a full-time job with one of her freelance clients, and started putting as much money toward her debts as possible. When her car broke down and she was on the verge of buying a new one, Scott convinced her not to take on any additional debt and loaned her an old car without air conditioning that he wasn't using.

When they got married, Karen still had a mountain of debt that Scott jokingly referred to as "a reverse dowry," but they tackled it together. Karen says, "I kept saying 'my debt, my debt,' but Scott would correct me and say it's 'our debt.'"

While it wasn't easy, they made the decision to wait until they were out of debt before buying a house. As they watched other friends buy multi-unit buildings with no money down, they thought they were missing out. But as the recession ravaged the real estate market, Scott and Karen came out of it in much better shape than most.

One other notable part of their story is that they tithed throughout their journey of getting out of debt. "Sometimes I would see our year-end giving statement, and I would say, 'Gee, we could have gotten out of debt so much faster if we had put that money toward our debts," Karen recalls. "I'd hear other people's stories of unexpected blessings that they felt came about because of their giving. I started wondering, *Where's my cool story?*"

Six and a half years after getting married, Scott and Karen made their last debt payment. It was a day neither one of them will ever forget. "It was amazing," Karen says. "We felt that it was a hard road we had traveled, but we did it, and we did it in a God-honoring way. We are 100 percent debt-free."

Scott will soon be able to retire with a full pension at a much younger age than most people, having put in more than twenty years as a Chicago firefighter. They're thinking about getting an RV and spending a year traveling the country. Sounds pretty cool to me.

THE HIGH PRICE OF DEBT

Living without debt is one of the best moves you can make for keeping financial stress in your marriage low. If you have any debt other than a reasonable mortgage, make it a high priority to get out (preferably before you get married), and then stay out, of debt.

Researcher Jeffrey Dew at Utah State University has found that "consumer debt (credit card debt and other installment loans) fuels a sense of financial unease among couples and increases the likelihood that they will fight over money matters; moreover, this financial unease casts a pall over marriages in general, raising the likelihood that couples will argue over issues other than money and decreasing the time they spend with one another."[1]

Dew's research shows that newlyweds who take on substantial consumer debt become less happy in their marriages over time. On the other hand, newly married couples who paid off their so-called consumer debt within their first five years of marriage reported being more satisfied with their marriage.[2] Those findings held up no matter whether couples were rich or poor.

Now for a four-step plan for getting and staying out of debt.

STEP ONE:
STOP GOING ANY FURTHER INTO DEBT

If you have debt other than a reasonable mortgage, mark today as the day you stop taking on more debt. In order to do so, make it as difficult as possible to go any further into debt. Take your credit cards out of your wallet or purse. Cut them up if you have to, or put them in a block of ice. Just get them out of reach.

Then tell a trusted friend or relative how much debt you have; tell the person that you're committed to getting out and staying out of debt; and invite him or her to pray for you, encourage you, and ask you about your progress from time to time.

It'll rearrange your bones to think about telling someone about your debt, but doing so will be one of the most helpful steps you can take to get out of debt. And do you know what else might happen? If you muster the courage to tell others about your debt, that just might create enough of a safe place for them to tell you about their debt too. You can be each other's accountability and encouragement partners.

If you're not married yet, keep in mind that this advice about not going any further into debt applies to your wedding. Having a nice, memorable wedding does not have to cost a fortune.

When I used Facebook and Twitter to ask for some recent examples of how people avoided going into wedding debt, Dawn wrote to say that she and her husband:

- Held their reception at the home of a relative
- Bought various items on eBay (veil, tiara, flower girl basket) and at Costco (beverages)

- Scheduled their wedding for early afternoon so that reception food consisted of heavy appetizers instead of a full meal
- Made their own wedding guest favors

Jan, who has helped several of her adult children with their weddings, recommended:

- Opting for a stand-up buffet instead of a sit-down meal
- Offering beer, wine, and soft drinks only (no open bar)
- Holding the wedding on a weeknight

Erin wrote with several money-saving ideas used at her own wedding, including:

- Designing her own wedding programs
- Having a relative make wedding favors

These women's ideas can help you put together a fantastic, *affordable* celebration.

Your wedding day will be one of the most important days of your life, and there is a lot of pressure to spend a fortune in a quest to make it especially memorable. I strongly recommend that to help you remember all of the great moments of your special day, you rely on the photographs, not several years' worth of credit card bills. For some additional ideas on cost-effective weddings, check the books and websites I recommend at www.MattAboutMoney.com (click on the "Resources" tab).

Now let's move on to the second of our four-part process for getting out of debt.

STEP TWO: REQUEST LOWER RATES

If you have always paid your bills on time, call the customer service number for each of your high-interest-rate credit cards and make this simple request: "I believe I've been a good customer, but I need a lower interest rate. Can you help me with that?" If they turn you down, ask to speak to a supervisor and repeat your request. It'll help if you have an offer in hand for a lower interest rate credit card. Be sure to mention that.

They may say no, but then again they may say yes, and an investment of ten to fifteen minutes of your time can have a great impact. Let's say you have a $2,000 balance on a credit card charging 18 percent interest and requiring a minimum payment of 2 percent of the balance. If you go no further into debt and pay the minimum amount required by the credit card company each month, it will take you more than twenty-four years to get out of debt, and you'll pay $4,400 in interest. Get your interest rate knocked down to 14 percent, and it'll bring your payoff date down to sixteen years and your interest payments down to $2,100. But we can easily do even better by taking the next step.

STEP THREE: FIX AND ROLL YOUR PAYMENTS

Did you know that credit card companies are incredibly generous? Consider this: If you have a balance you're carrying from month to month, you don't go any further into debt, and you make the monthly minimum-required payments, then that required payment amount will decrease each month. Isn't that kind of the credit card company? Of course, it isn't generosity; it's math. Your minimum-required payment is based on a percentage of your balance, so if your balance declines a little each month, your required payment will decline a little as well. Paying this declining minimum amount will keep you in debt for approximately forever.

A much better plan is to fix your payments. Take note of this month's required payment amount, and then next month when a smaller payment is required, thank them for their generosity but send them the same amount you sent this month. After all, if you can afford to pay that amount this month, you can probably afford to pay the same amount next month. Depending on how much debt you have, just fixing your payments will speed up the process of getting out of debt by years and save you thousands of dollars in interest.

In our previous example, if you fix your payments on that $2,000 of debt, you will go from a sixteen-year payoff period to little over a six-year payoff period, and your interest payments will go from over $2,000 to $1,000. Wow! Reducing the interest rate helped some, but fixing your payments helped a lot.

If you have multiple debts, once the first one is paid off, take the full amount you were paying toward that debt and roll it into the fixed amount you've been paying on your next-lowest-balance debt. Keep repeating this procedure for as many debts as you have. The only debt I don't have a big issue with is a mortgage, as long as it's reasonable (more on that in chapter 13).

··

Should I Transfer My Balance to a 0 Percent Interest Credit Card?

I'm generally not in favor of transferring balances to a 0 percent interest credit card for the following reasons:

- For the privilege, you'll usually pay a hefty fee based on a percentage of the amount being transferred.
- The 0 percent interest rate is usually for a limited amount of time.
- If you're late with a payment, your interest rate skyrockets.
- The time and energy you spend moving your debt around would be best spent managing your expenses so you can free up money to accelerate your payments.

··

STEP FOUR: ACCELERATE YOUR PAYMENTS

If you can pay more than the fixed minimum payment, you'll be out of debt even faster. Fix your payments for all of your debts, but add an accelerator amount to your lowest-balance debt. Once that is paid off, take the full amount you were paying on it and roll it over into the next-lowest-balance debt.

In our $2,000 debt example, instead of paying a fixed $40 each month, what if you were able to double that to $80? Now your payoff period drops from a little over six years to just two and a half years, and your interest payments drop from $1,000 to just $380.

On my website (www.MattAboutMoney.com), you'll find a calculator that'll help you see how much more quickly you'll be out of debt if you add another $10, $50, $100, or more. Running your numbers may motivate you to come up with as much money as possible to speed up the process of getting out of debt.

The Great Low-Balance/High-Interest-Rate Debate

I'm often asked which is best—to apply an accelerator to the lowest-balance or the highest-interest-rate debt? Either way is fine, but I generally recommend going after the lowest-balance debt first. It's true that people will typically get out of debt *a little bit* faster and will pay *a little bit* less interest by tackling their highest-interest-rate debts first. However, by going after your lowest-balance debt first, you will usually get one of your debts paid off faster than if you had gone after the highest-interest-rate debt. Getting a win under your belt quickly feels good. It will give you the motivation to stick with the plan.

A couple of specific types of debt warrant their own instruction. Let's start with vehicle debt.

VEHICLE DEBT

Unfortunately, many people assume they will always have a vehicle payment. How else will they be able to drive the latest-model car with all the new features? But driving vehicles that aren't hitched to a loan is one of the most important keys to a life of financial freedom. That doesn't mean you have to drive the oldest car on the block. If you buy vehicles that are one or two years old, keep them for at least another eight years, and regularly put money into a savings account earmarked for your next car, you will spend far less on transportation than the average person.

If you currently have a vehicle loan, pay it off as quickly as you can. Once you are out of vehicle debt, keep making the payments. Just send them to your savings account instead of your finance company. If you do that, you should have plenty of money saved up to buy your next car with cash.

....

What About Buying a Car Offered at 0 Percent Financing?

I'm generally opposed to these "deals." The only way it may work is as follows:

- **You have and will maintain the full amount you owe on the car in savings for as long as you are making payments.** Otherwise, you are presuming upon the future, which Scripture cautions against (see Proverbs 27:1; James 4:13-15).
- **You've done the research and determined that the purchase price really is a good deal.** Oftentimes, it is not. The price has been marked up to allow for the fact that the dealer isn't making any money on financing.
- **You're planning to keep the car for at least ten years.** Cars depreciate quickly, which is why it is usually a better deal to buy a car that is one or two years old. However, if

you are planning to keep the vehicle a long time, you
might come out ahead having bought new, as you would
have the full warranty and there are no hidden mechanical
problems created by the previous owner.

....

STUDENT LOAN DEBT

At a premarriage financial workshop I was leading, I met a couple who
clearly disagreed about how to handle their education debts. The man
was still in law school, and he was content to make the minimum payments on more than $100,000 of student loan debts after they got
married. He assumed he would land a well-paid job at a law firm, and
the monthly debt payments would take just a small fraction of his salary. He was eager to buy a nice condominium after they got married.
She wanted to live more modestly for their first few years, focus as
much money as they could on getting out of debt, and then increase
their lifestyle spending.

I encouraged them to pay off the debt before taking on a big mortgage, but he didn't seem persuaded. If I'd had more time, I would have
asked him if I could talk with him privately for a few minutes and I
would have told him it would be an amazing act of service—an act of
love, really—if he would wait before buying the expensive condo. His
student loan was clearly a concern to his fiancée. Besides, there's no way
of knowing for sure how one's career is going to work out.

If you have student loans, put them on the repayment fast track.
Wiping them out as soon as possible, even if that means having to live
more frugally than you would like to for a few years, will give you great
financial freedom.

What if you're in a different position, such as struggling even to
make the minimum-required payments on your student loans? If you
are out of work or have gone back to school, you may be able to have
your loan payments deferred. If you're working but your student loan

payments require a lot of your income, you may be eligible for an income-based repayment plan, which is available for most federal student loans and caps your monthly payments at a level designed to be affordable for someone with your income and family size. If you work for a governmental agency or nonprofit, you may even be eligible to have the remaining balance of your loan forgiven after making payments for ten years under a public service loan forgiveness program. Check the website www.studentaid.ed.gov to learn more about both programs.

Here's one final note about education loans: If you have a student loan and you move after getting married, make sure the company that services your loan has your new address. It is not uncommon for young married couples to have difficulty obtaining a mortgage because one partner has been missing student loan payments because of failing to give the company processing the loan an updated address.

COMMIT TO FINANCIAL FREEDOM

Carrying a heavy load of debt is so common in our culture that it feels normal, unavoidable. It might be normal, but it is not healthy. Commit from the beginning of your marriage to being one of those unusual couples who carries no debt other than a reasonable mortgage and you will be unusually free.

TAKE ACTION

What to Do
Fill in the "Debts" section of the *Cash Flow Plan* on page 64. If you have multiple debts, transfer to the "Goal" column the *fixed* payment you are making on each one except the lowest balance debt. For that one, set a goal of an accelerator amount you will begin adding to the fixed minimum payment.

What to Discuss

- If you aren't married yet and have debt, what can you do to speed up the process of getting out of debt? What would it take to be completely debt-free by your wedding date?
- If you are engaged, how committed are you to not going into debt for your wedding? What steps can you take to avoid borrowing for your wedding?
- Will it be a priority in your marriage not to finance vehicles?
- If you are already married and have debt, what action steps will you take to get out of debt as soon as possible?
- If either of you has student loan debt, how much of a priority is it to fast-track its repayment?

CHAPTER 10

MANAGE YOUR CREDIT SCORE

A good name is more desirable than great riches; to be esteemed is better than silver or gold.

PROVERBS 22:1

It takes many good deeds to build a good reputation, and only one bad one to lose it.

BENJAMIN FRANKLIN

FINANCIALLY, YOUR REPUTATION BOILS down to a three-digit number: your credit score. It doesn't matter what people *say* about how responsible you are with money; what matters is how responsible you *actually are*, especially in managing your use of credit. Each credit-related action you take is recorded, tallied, and turned into your credit score.

A good credit score will help you get the best rate on a mortgage and a lot more. Insurers, cell phone providers, and a growing list of other companies base their decisions about working with you and at what rates, in part, on your credit report and/or score. More and more landlords and employers are checking the same information before

<109>

renting you a place to live or hiring you.

There is no such thing as a joint credit report or score. Your credit information is tied to your Social Security number, so the act of getting married will not impact your credit report or score.

However, if you apply for a mortgage or any other form of credit together, both of your scores will be used in determining whether lenders will work with you and what rates they will charge. Clearly, knowing your scores and keeping them as strong as possible is important.

Here's what you can do to successfully manage your credit score.

PAY YOUR BILLS ON TIME

Thirty-five percent of your credit score is based on your track record of paying your bills on schedule. Do all that you can to pay your bills on time. Most credit card companies and many utilities will send you an e-mail alert a week or so before your next payment is due. Sign up for these free alerts. If you are using an online budget tool such as Mint, it will send you alerts as well.

BE CAREFUL ABOUT HOW MUCH CREDIT YOU USE

Thirty percent of your credit score is based on how much you owe. What is especially important is how much of your available credit you are using ("credit utilization") across all of your credit cards and on each individual card. Using 30 percent of your available credit or less is good; 10 percent or less is ideal. This goes for people who pay their balances in full each month, not just those who carry a balance.

GIVE IT TIME

Fifteen percent of your credit score is determined by how long you have used credit.

I'm often asked in workshops whether to close old, unused accounts. This is generally not a good idea, but not because doing so will erase your credit history. Even if you closed an account, positive information about the account would stay on your report for ten years, negative information for seven years.

The problem with closing an old account has to do with credit utilization. Closing an account lowers your total available credit, which may increase your utilization, and that can lower your credit score.

BE CAUTIOUS ABOUT OPENING NEW ACCOUNTS

The amount of credit you have applied for recently impacts 10 percent of your score. Opening new credit card accounts as you make your way through the mall in order to get all those 10 percent discounts on your purchases tends to discount your credit score.

USE VARIOUS TYPES OF CREDIT

Your mix of installment loans, revolving credit, and/or a mortgage is an important part of the final 10 percent of your score. Having some of each type of credit is ideal. Installment loans are those with a fixed payoff period, such as a vehicle or student loan. Revolving loans are open-ended loans, such as credit cards. However, I don't recommend taking on new loans just for the purpose of trying to improve your credit score.

REVIEW YOUR FREE CREDIT REPORT

Everyone is entitled to one free report each year from each of the three credit bureaus: Experian, Equifax, and TransUnion. Get your reports at www.annualcreditreport.com. Here's what to look for in each of their major sections:

- **Credit summary**. Toward the top of your Equifax report, under "Accounts," you will see your credit utilization, or what is called debt-to-available-credit ratio. This is the area you can do something about to impact your score the most in the least amount of time.

  If you have a high debt-to-available-credit ratio, you will raise your score if you can pay down your debt, especially credit card debt. The improvement should show up within thirty days.

- **Account information**. Are there any accounts you don't recognize? This could be a sign of identity theft. If you see such accounts, contact those creditors directly and let them know that the accounts are not yours.

  Also, under account information, check to see if there are any accounts listed as open that are actually closed. Review your credit limits and compare them to the limits stated on your credit card statements. If the report lists your credit limits as being lower than they really are, your credit utilization will be incorrectly high.

  Check to see if there are any late payments noted. For Experian, you want your open account status listed as "Open/ Never Late." For Equifax, "Pays as Agreed." For TransUnion, "Paid or Paying as Agreed." If any accounts are listed otherwise and you believe that you have never been late with a payment, contact the creditor. Even if you don't have proof that you paid on time, let them know that you believe a mistake has been made and ask if they will change it on your credit file.

- **Inquiries**. An inquiry occurs anytime anyone checks your credit report. A "hard inquiry" occurs when you apply for credit and the prospective lender checks your credit report or score. Lots of recent hard inquiries will work against you.

  "Soft inquiries" come from lenders looking to make you a preapproved credit offer, existing creditors reviewing your file, prospective employers and insurers, or yourself when you check your own report. These do not hurt your credit score.

- **Negative information**. If you filed for bankruptcy more than ten years ago, this should no longer be showing up on your report.
- **Personal information**. Check to see that the following information is correct: the spelling of your name, your birth date, current and previous addresses, Social Security number, and current and past employer information.

If you see any problems on your report, file a dispute. Instructions are on your report. Make copies of forms you fill out and any responses you get. The bureaus must investigate your dispute within thirty days unless they deem it to be frivolous.

GUARD AGAINST IDENTITY THEFT

The single best step you can take to guard against identity theft is to zealously guard your Social Security number. If someone steals your credit card number, they can run up charges on your account, but chances are good that the credit card company won't make you pay. On the other hand, if someone gets your Social Security number, they can open new accounts in your name, which you might not discover for months or even years.

Only a handful of organizations have a legitimate need to know your number. They include: your employer, your bank and brokerage house, and your doctor. If someone else asks you for your Social Security number, double-check with his or her supervisor to see if it is truly necessary. And then you may need to talk with *that* person's supervisor. A cell phone service provider told one person I know that a Social Security number was required. It took talking with eight different people to find out that a driver's license number could be used instead.

DO THE RIGHT THING

Credit scores have an aura of mystery. There's no end to the articles offering this strategy or that for increasing one's score. The truth is, there are two basic steps everyone can take to build and maintain a good score: Pay your bills on time and use a relatively small amount of your available credit. Focusing on those two things will go a long way toward keeping your financial reputation—your credit score—strong.

TAKE ACTION

What to Do

In chapter 2, I had you pull your free credit reports and buy your credit score. Now use the information in this chapter to review your reports to look for any inaccuracies. If you find any, take the recommended steps to get the problems fixed.

What to Discuss

- What are some steps you could take to make sure you never pay bills late?
- Have you signed up to receive e-mail alerts reminding you when bill payments are due?
- What percentage of the available credit on your credit cards do you typically use each month? Is it higher than 10%? Is it higher than 30%? If so, what can you do to reduce your credit utilization?

CHAPTER 11

PATIENTLY PURSUE INTEREST

Dishonest money dwindles away, but he who gathers money little by little makes it grow.

PROVERBS 13:11

October: This is one of the peculiarly dangerous months to speculate in stocks. The others are July, January, September, April, November, May, March, June, December, August, and February.

MARK TWAIN

CONSIDER THE FOLLOWING SCENARIOS.

When Frank and Sandy were twenty-five years old, they scraped together $200 per month and invested that money in a way that generated an average annual return of 8 percent. However, when they turned age thirty-five, they had to start helping their elderly parents and could no longer make those investments. Because they didn't need to touch the money they had invested, they left it where it could continue earning 8 percent per year. When they turned seventy, their $24,000 ($2,400 invested each year for ten years) had grown to $600,000.

<115>

Now compare them to Joe and Karen. When they were twenty-five years old, they found it impossible to come up with any money to invest. But they figured they were young and there'd be plenty of time for that later. They decided to begin investing when they turned thirty-five and invested $200 per month until they were seventy years old, along the way earning 8 percent each year. After thirty-five years of investing $200 per month—a total of $84,000—their nest egg totaled just $462,000. They invested *more than three times* as much as Frank and Sandy had and yet ended up with nearly $140,000 less.

As these stories show, when you're young you stand to gain the most from the power of compound interest, the process whereby invested money earns interest, and that interest earns interest, and on and on. Make it a priority to begin investing a portion of all you earn early in your marriage, and you will likely end up in your later years with a nest egg that can generate enough interest to live on comfortably.

The principles in this chapter are designed to teach you how to invest successfully. However, keep in mind that the order of the chapters in this section is intentional. Before beginning to invest, you should be giving generously, have six months' worth of living expenses in an emergency fund, be out of debt other than a reasonable mortgage, and be saving for goals to be accomplished within the next five years. If that's your situation, here are your next steps.

DETERMINE GOALS TO BE ACCOMPLISHED IN THE NEXT FIVE-PLUS YEARS

What turns a savings goal into an investment goal is how much time you have to accomplish your goal. If you have less than five years, you should put goal money into a savings or money market account, a money market mutual fund, or a CD, as described in chapter 8. If you have more than five years, you are starting to move into the realm of investing and can generally afford to be more aggressive in pursuit of a higher rate of return. For a goal to be accomplished in the next five to ten years, you might consider putting money into a balanced mutual fund, a type of fund offered by most of the big mutual fund companies that is typically invested 50 to 60 percent in bonds and 40 to 50 percent in stocks. For some online tools that can help you choose specific funds, check my website at www.MattAboutMoney.com.

If you have more than ten years to invest, you can be even more aggressive. Here are the foundational investing principles you need to understand and incorporate into your investment plans.

RECOGNIZE THE RISKS

The more time you have to accomplish a financial goal, the more risk you can afford to take. The more risk you are willing to take, the greater your *potential* for earning a higher rate of return.

As we saw in chapter 1, chances are good that you and your fiancé/fiancée or spouse view risk through different filters. One person in each couple is usually more comfortable taking risks than the other. However, living at either extreme of the risk spectrum will not be good for your money or your marriage. If you are overly conservative, preferring to "invest" in only CDs, you will probably never have enough to pay for your later years. The interest generated by CDs is simply unlikely to beat the rate of inflation. In that sense, playing it too safe may end up being the riskiest thing you could do. On the other hand, if you are too adventurous with your investments, you risk taking huge losses and fraying the nerves of your mate.

If you each stand on opposite ends of the risk spectrum, following the principles in this chapter should help you move toward each other, and that's important. While retirement accounts are held in your individual names, you should agree with what the other is investing in. After all, the performance of your retirement accounts will impact both of you.

If you can't reconcile your different appetites for risk, one solution may be to use a financial advisor. Interview several so you're both comfortable with the one you choose. Then let that person guide your investment decisions. A good advisor will help you strike the right balance between your different risk-tolerance levels while choosing investments appropriate for your age and goals. On my website, I list a couple of other sites that will help you find a good advisor. Under a typical arrangement, the advisor will charge a fee based on a percentage of the assets you turn over for his or her management, often around 1 percent.

Whether making your own investment choices or working with an advisor, care should be taken to determine your investment needs.

KNOW YOUR NEEDS

Less than half of all of today's workers have taken the time to estimate how much they should be investing each month in order to meet their retirement goals. Those who have taken this step feel more confident about their ability to fund their retirement.[1]

To estimate how much you need to invest in order to fund your retirement, use Fidelity's Retirement Quick Check. (Go to www.fidelity .com and search for "Retirement Quick Check." If you don't have a Fidelity account, you'll need to register as a Fidelity member.) After about thirty minutes of answering questions, you'll find out the total amount of money you are likely to need when you step out of the paid workforce and how much you need to invest each month, starting now.

DIVERSIFY

This foundational principle for wise investing has its roots in Scripture. King Solomon, the richest man of his day (and quite possibly the richest man who ever lived), said, "Cast your bread upon the waters, for you will find it after many days. Give a portion to seven, or even to eight, for you know not what disaster may happen on earth" (Ecclesiastes 11:1-2, esv). In this passage, Solomon talks about spreading one's generosity among the many in need. That way, if you become needy, one of those whom you helped may be able and willing to help you. He was recommending diversification of your generosity dollars; it's a timeless principle for wise investing as well.

In order to properly diversify your investments, most people will be better off investing in mutual funds rather than individual stocks. Choosing the right stocks takes time and specialized knowledge. Plus, in order to be properly diversified, you need to invest in a variety of stocks. With mutual funds, you get instant diversification. A single mutual fund is typically invested in many different stocks, bonds, or other investments. Still, there are a lot of mutual funds to choose from. How do you know which are best for you?

First, decide whether to invest in actively managed mutual funds or in index funds. With an actively managed fund, an investment manager chooses investments, making many buying and selling decisions throughout the year. While there are some great mutual fund mangers, most fail to beat the benchmarks against which the performance of their funds is measured.[2]

That's one reason why I prefer index funds. An index fund is set up to mirror one of many indices, such as the S&P 500 (a composite of large-company stocks) or the Russell 2000 (a composite of small-company stocks). The investments held in an index fund mirror those that make up the index it emulates, and in the same proportion. I also like index funds because they have lower costs than actively managed mutual funds. Even no-load (sales charge) mutual funds have expenses, which eat into their investment returns. Index funds typically have much lower expenses than actively managed funds.

The next principle will help you determine what types of index funds to invest in.

ALLOCATE PROPERLY

According to John Bogle, founder of Vanguard Mutual Funds, "Asset allocation is almost universally considered the most important determinant of your long-term investment return."[3] Asset allocation has to do with what percentages of your investments are in stocks, bonds, and other types of investments.

To determine the proper asset allocation for you, you could use an asset allocation calculator (you'll find my latest recommendation for the best asset allocation calculator on my website at www .MattAboutMoney.com/resources), which will use factors such as your age, current investments, and risk tolerance to calculate what percentage of your investment portfolio should be in each asset class. From there, it's up to you to choose the actual mutual funds.

Or you could choose a so-called target-date mutual fund. Such funds offer preset asset allocations, often investing in other mutual funds that the company offering the target-date fund believes are best for someone with your retirement date in mind. If you plan to retire in forty-five years, the target-date fund designed around that goal will probably feature an aggressive mix of mostly stock mutual funds and a much smaller allotment of bond funds. As you get older, the allocation will automatically change, becoming more conservative as you get closer to your intended retirement date.

With a target-date fund, you choose a fund that includes in its name the approximate year of your intended retirement. For instance, let's say you plan to retire in 2050. You could put money into Vanguard's target-date fund for that year, called Target Retirement 2050; Fidelity's, which is called Fidelity Freedom 2050; or another mutual fund company's target-date fund.

While most of the big mutual fund companies offer target-date funds, all target-date funds are not created equal. Some use more aggressive assumptions than others, so it's wise to compare the asset allocations used by several mutual fund companies recommended by an unbiased source such as *Consumer Reports*.

Whether you choose your own mutual funds, go with a target-date fund, or invest through an advisor, it's impossible to know whether the market will be up or down this month or next. That's why I recommend investing a set amount at the same time every month, a process known as dollar cost averaging. When the market is down, your dollars buy more mutual fund shares; when it's up, your dollars buy fewer shares.

There are also numerous tax-advantaged ways to invest for your future. Let's look at some of the main options if you work for someone else and if you work for yourself.

MANAGE TAXES

Note: All contribution limits are based on the rules and regulations for 2010. Check my website for the latest limits.

Options for Employees

If your employer offers a retirement plan, here are your main choices.

Traditional 401(k), 403(b), and 457(b) plans. Corporations, nonprofits, and government agencies offer these retirement plans. Typically, these plans allow you to contribute up to $16,500 of your salary. If you are fifty or older, you can contribute an additional $5,500. If you have a high income, you may face additional restrictions on how much you can contribute.

Money you contribute to any of these plans goes in pretax. The interest earned is tax-deferred, and you will pay income taxes on the money when you withdraw it. You must keep this money in the plan until at least age fifty-nine and a half in order to avoid early withdrawal penalties and taxes, and you must begin taking withdrawals by age seventy and a half, at the latest. You can borrow against such plans, but if you leave your employer, you will have to repay the loan within a short amount of time.

Roth 401(k), 403(b), and 457(b) plans. The main differences between a traditional and a Roth workplace retirement plan are that with a Roth, the money you contribute goes in after you've paid taxes on it, the earnings grow tax-free, and then the money you withdraw comes out tax-free. If your employer offers you a choice between a traditional and a Roth retirement plan, it may be more beneficial to go with the Roth plan, especially if you believe that you will be in a higher tax bracket when you reach retirement age. Or you could hedge your bets as to whether you'll be in a higher or lower tax bracket by the time you retire by splitting your contributions between the plans.

One especially nice feature of workplace Roth plans is that whereas there are income restrictions governing eligibility for a Roth IRA, there are no such restrictions for participating in a workplace Roth.

Non-Workplace Options

Traditional IRA. With this type of IRA, money is contributed before-tax, earnings grow on a tax-deferred basis, and withdrawals beginning at age fifty-nine and a half are taxable. If neither of you participates in a workplace retirement plan and you are forty-nine years old or younger, you may each make tax-deductible contributions of up to $5,000 per year into a traditional IRA, $6,000 if you are fifty or older.

If you both participate in a workplace plan and file a joint income tax return, you may contribute to an IRA, but your contributions will be fully deductible only if your adjusted gross income (AGI) is less than $89,000. You may make partially deductible contributions if your AGI is between $89,000 and $109,000, at which point contributions become nondeductible.

The same deductibility limits apply to a spouse who participates in an employer plan when the other does not, again as long as you file a joint return.

For a spouse who does not participate in an employer plan when the other does, the income thresholds are higher. Deductibility of contributions begins to phase out when household income hits $167,000, with deductibility completely phased out when AGI is $177,000 or higher.

Roth IRA. With this type of IRA, money is contributed after tax, earnings grow tax-free, and withdrawals starting at age fifty-nine and a half are tax-free.

There are no eligibility restrictions related to your participation in a workplace plan. However, there are income restrictions.

As long as you file a joint income tax return and your household AGI is less than $167,000, you can contribute up to $5,000 per year if you are forty-nine years old or younger and up to $6,000 if you are fifty or older. You may make partial contributions if your AGI is between $167,000 and less than $177,000, at which point you become ineligible to contribute to a Roth.

A Roth IRA offers numerous benefits over a traditional IRA:

- You can access your money more easily. Contributions may be withdrawn at any time for any reason with no penalty (this is not true with a workplace Roth).
- You can withdraw earnings after five years as long as the money is used for specific purposes, including a first-time home purchase and qualifying education expenses (again, not true with a workplace Roth).
- You don't have to withdraw money when you reach age seventy and a half (this is the same as a workplace Roth), and you may continue to make contributions to a Roth past age seventy and a half as long as you have earned income.

Still, other factors may make a traditional IRA more advantageous for you than a Roth. To help determine which type makes the most sense for you, see my website for my latest recommendation for the best Roth versus Traditional IRA calculator.

Spousal IRA. If only one of you is in the paid workforce, the other spouse may still be eligible for an IRA (traditional or Roth) if you file your income taxes jointly. The non-paid spouse may contribute $5,000 per year ($6,000 if he or she is fifty or older), as long as the paid spouse has enough earned income to cover the contribution. If the working spouse participates in a workplace retirement plan, there is one added restriction: His or her AGI must be below $167,000 in order for the non-paid spouse to make a deductible contribution to a traditional IRA. Partially deductible contributions may be made if the AGI is below $177,000. At that level or above, the non-paid spouse may still contribute to a traditional IRA, but none of the contribution would be deductible. If the working spouse does not participate in a qualified retirement plan, there are no deductibility restrictions on contributions to a traditional IRA. The other income restrictions noted in the Traditional IRA and Roth IRA sections previously discussed also apply.

My recommendation. If your employer offers a retirement plan and matches a portion of your contributions, contribute the amount needed to take full advantage of that match. For example, if your employer will match up to 3 percent of your salary, contribute 3 percent of your salary to your workplace plan.

Next, if you meet the income restrictions, open and contribute the maximum to a Roth IRA. If, based on the amount you decide to invest for your later years, you still have money to invest, go back to your workplace plan and contribute more there. If you do not qualify for a Roth IRA, contribute the maximum to your workplace plan.

If your employer offers a plan without a match and you are eligible to contribute to a Roth IRA, start there. If after maxing out your contribution you still have money to invest for your retirement, contribute to your workplace plan. If you're not eligible for a Roth IRA, you'll have to stick with your workplace plan.

If your employer does not offer a plan, you'll have to go with a traditional or Roth IRA. Again, use the calculator recommended on my site to determine which one is best for you.

Options for the Self-Employed

If you are self-employed, here are two good options for investing for your retirement.

SEP-IRA. Otherwise known as a Simplified Employee Pension Plan, a SEP-IRA allows self-employed people to sock away a lot of money for retirement without a lot of paperwork. The contribution limits vary based on your business structure. If you own an S or C corporation, an incorporated partnership, or an LLC, the business may contribute up to 25 percent of your salary up to $49,000. If you are a sole proprietor, a maximum 20 percent of your salary may be contributed up to the same limit.

Solo 401(k). This type of plan allows you to save even more for your retirement. You may contribute 100 percent of your first $16,500 in salary or sole proprietorship income each year up to age fifty ($22,500 per year if you are fifty or older), plus 25 percent of your salary or 20 percent of sole proprietorship income. Total contributions cap out at $49,000, or $54,500 if you are fifty or older. This plan requires more paperwork than a SEP-IRA and can be more expensive to administer, and if you have employees, you may need to contribute to their 401(k) accounts as well.

Even though the maximum contribution to a Solo 401(k) is the same as with a SEP-IRA ($49,000), unless your salary is extremely high, you will often come out ahead with a Solo 401(k). For example, let's say you have a C corporation and pay yourself $80,000 per year. With a SEP, you can contribute $20,000 (25 percent of $80,000). However, with a Solo 401(k), you can contribute $36,500 ($16,500 plus $20,000).

....

Investing for College

If and when you have children, you will need to decide whether to help them pay for college. College might seem like a long way off, but just as with retirement funding, you'll be able to accumulate more money at a lower cost if you start earlier.

A great calculator for figuring out how much to invest each month is on the appropriately named website www.SavingForCollege.com. The site also has helpful information about the various ways you can save for such expenses, and it rates the various versions of one of the most popular college investment tools, a 529 plan. If you opt for a 529 plan offered by your state, in most cases you get a state

income tax deduction. Earnings are tax-free, and the
money comes out tax-free as long as it is used for qualified education expenses.

....

GET IN THE INVESTMENT GAME
AS SOON AS POSSIBLE

Making wise investment choices requires an investment of time, but
don't let that keep you on the sidelines. Remember, the earlier you
begin, the more you'll be able to maximize the power of compound
interest, so use the principles in this chapter and get started. In the next
chapter, we'll switch from offense to defense, determining how to
choose the right types and amounts of insurance to carry.

TAKE ACTION

What to Do
Fill in the "Goal" column of the "Retirement" line in the "Investing"
section of the *Cash Flow Plan* on page 64. Do you need to make
any changes relative to the amount you are now investing each
month? If you have never estimated your retirement needs, run the
analysis using the calculator recommended earlier.

What to Discuss
- Aside from your retirement, are there any other goals you'd like
  to accomplish five or more years from now that you should be
  investing for?
- How has this chapter helped you reconcile any differences
  between your investment styles or risk tolerances?
- If one of you plans to step out of the paid workforce at some
  point, should you be doing anything differently, such as investing
  a higher percentage of your salaries, in order to prepare for that?

- Of the investment approaches mentioned—choosing your own mutual funds, using a target-date fund, or working with an investment advisor—which one appeals to you and why?
- If you plan to choose your own investments, which one of you has the better track record as an investor? Will that person take the lead in recommending investments once you are married?
- Up to now, how much thought have you given to your asset allocation? What changes do you need to make?

CHAPTER 12

BUILD WALLS OF PROTECTION

The prudent see danger and take refuge, but the simple keep going and suffer for it.

PROVERBS 27:12

Let the fear of a danger be a spur to prevent it; he that fears not gives advantage to the danger.

BENJAMIN DISRAELI

NO ONE HAS EVER accused an insurance policy of being a page-turner. However, those packets of boring legalese are essential for financial success. While a well-stocked emergency fund will protect you against relatively small or short-lived financial problems, insurance provides the necessary protections against bigger or longer-lasting problems. Let's look at the kinds of insurance available so that you can determine what kinds of insurance you should have and how much.

<129>

LIFE INSURANCE

Do You Need It?

The easiest way to answer this question is to consider whether anyone would suffer financially if you died. You may not need life insurance if both you and your spouse are working full-time and neither of you has an ex-spouse or children from a previous marriage. If one of you died today, the other may be able to handle his or her financial obligations. Still, there are some reasons to consider buying life insurance now:

- **If you have financial obligations that require both of your incomes**. I don't recommend buying a house that requires both of your incomes, as I explain in the next chapter, but if you're in that situation already, you may want to have enough life insurance to be able to pay off the mortgage or to pay it down so it could be refinanced and afforded by the surviving spouse.

- **If you want to protect against the possibility that one or both of you could become medically uninsurable in the future**. If you developed some type of illness while you did not have life insurance, you may not be able to get a policy. Buying a policy while you're healthy guards against that scenario.

- **If you want to lock in the lowest rates**. Premiums for life insurance will typically go up as you get older. Buy policies now, and you'll lock in the lower cost. Of course, you'll also pay premiums for a longer period of time. You have to weigh the pros and cons.

- **If you don't have much money in savings**. You may want enough life insurance to cover funeral and other final expenses.

- **If you have debts that would be difficult to pay off without two incomes**. Credit card debt held in one spouse's name does not necessarily absolve the other from the obligation to pay it off. In a community property state, a spouse's debts incurred after getting married may be the responsibility of the other spouse as well; state laws vary. In states not governed by community property law, many creditors will write off the debts of a deceased person when he or she held the credit card in his or her name only. But not always. In some states, if the credit card debt was accrued through purchases of items that benefited the family, a surviving spouse may be held responsible for those debts.

Once you have children, the question quickly shifts from "Do we need life insurance?" to "How much life insurance do we need?"

How Much Do We Need?

You'll hear about various guidelines for estimating how much insurance to carry based on multiples of your salary. Some say you should carry insurance with a death benefit equal to ten times your salary. But this is a broad-brush approach. It's better to take time to consider how much you really need.

Either run a detailed analysis using a life insurance needs calculator, such as the one found at www.lifehappens.org, or follow this streamlined process recommended by *Consumer Reports*.[1]

1. Estimate your current monthly living expenses: $_____
2. Estimate your family's future monthly living expenses assuming you are no longer living: $_____ (Multiplying the amount from line one by .75 should give you a reasonable estimate.)
3. Estimate your surviving spouse's future monthly income, including earned income, investment income, rental property income, and Social Security survivor's benefits (www .socialsecurity.gov): $_____
4. Subtract line 3 from line 2: $_____ (This is your monthly shortfall that you'll want to cover with insurance.)

5. Multiply the figure on line 4 by the number of months your survivors will need to cover the shortfall: $_____ (Let's say you came up with a $3,000 monthly shortfall in line 4 and you wanted to cover this need until a newborn reaches age eighteen. You would multiply $3,000 by 216 (12 months multiplied by 18 years) and come up with a needed death benefit of $648,000.)

I recommend one more step: Add any other expenses you would want to cover in the event of your untimely death, such as a child's future college expenses.

Whether you run a detailed analysis or use the simplified approach above, the death benefit you come up with assumes you will use up the life insurance proceeds as you spend them. In the example I just described, after eighteen years of covering the $3,000 monthly shortfall with life insurance proceeds, the entire $648,000 would be gone. Actually, you would likely earn some interest in that time, but the assumption behind this type of needs assessment is that you will use the principal of the proceeds to pay expenses.

Another approach is to have enough life insurance so that if it were invested conservatively, the interest alone would cover the survivor's needs; the principal could stay invested. In order to generate $3,000 each month on an ongoing basis through interest income, assuming you could earn a 5 percent return on your investment of the insurance proceeds, you would need a policy with a death benefit of $720,000. A $720,000 policy would not cost all that much more than a $648,000 policy and you would be further securing your survivors' financial future.

Once you know how much monthly income you would need to cover through life insurance and for how long, estimate the total death benefit needed both ways — using the principal to cover the need versus conservatively investing it and using the interest to cover the need — and then compare the costs of buying the different amounts of insurance. You may decide it's worth the added cost to buy enough life insurance to cover your survivors' needs through investment interest.

Be sure to estimate life insurance needs for both of you. Even if one spouse is not in the paid workforce, if you have minor children, it makes sense to cover that spouse with life insurance. One approach is to cover that person for the cost of any services the surviving partner would have to pay for until the youngest child is on his or her own, such as child care and perhaps housekeeping.

In our household, Jude is home taking care of our kids and managing our household full-time. We agree that if something happened to her, we would want me to be more freed up from my work responsibilities to focus on raising our kids. We want enough insurance so that conservatively investing the death benefit would provide enough income for me to at least go down to a part-time work schedule.

Which Type Should We Get?

The two main types of life insurance are term and permanent life insurance.

Term life insurance. Term life insurance is pure insurance, covers a temporary need, and is the least expensive type of life insurance. By "pure insurance," I mean you pay for the death benefit and nothing more. Term insurance covers you for a specific period of time, typically ranging from one to thirty years, hence the name *term*.

Couples often choose term insurance in order to protect against their premature deaths while their kids are younger than eighteen or perhaps until they are done with college. The couples assume that by that point they won't need life insurance anymore; they will have been diligent in saving and investing all those years and will have enough assets to provide for the surviving spouse. This philosophy is usually described as "buy term and invest the difference." You just need to make sure you don't buy term and *spend* the difference!

If you go the term route, it's generally best to choose a level-premium policy, which means you will pay the same amount every year for the term of the policy. Also, ask whether the policy is convertible.

Convertible policies give you the option to convert the policy to a permanent life insurance policy without having to take a medical test.

Permanent life insurance. This type of insurance, also called whole life, gives you a death benefit and a savings or investment account, provides permanent coverage (assuming you keep up with the premiums), and is much more expensive than term life insurance. Whereas a term policy might cost you roughly $15 to $30 per month per $100,000 of death benefit, a permanent life policy could cost $150 to $300 per month.

Young couples with kids usually need a lot of insurance and have many other expenses. For those reasons, term is often the most viable way to get the coverage you need at a price you can afford. But there are some circumstances where a permanent life insurance policy may make sense.

If you are contributing the maximum amount into eligible tax-advantaged retirement accounts, you may want to consider a permanent life insurance policy. While the money you pay in premiums goes in after you've paid income taxes on it, the money in the policy's cash account grows on a tax-deferred basis.

When you retire and want to use some of the cash value for living expenses, there are even ways to take that money out of the policy without paying income taxes. For example, you can borrow the money, with the loan repaid by a portion of the death benefit upon your death. Dividends earned from the policy may be sufficient to cover the interest payments on the loan. If not, you could pay the interest out of pocket or allow the death benefit to be further reduced by the owed interest.

You could also convert the cash value in the policy to an annuity that pays income for the rest of your life.

If a portion of your estate may be subject to estate taxes upon your deaths, you may want to consider a permanent life insurance policy as well. You may pay far less in premiums than your estate would owe in taxes, enabling you to leave more of your estate to your heirs or charities.

One other benefit of a permanent life insurance policy is that at a certain point, no more premium payments are required. Either the policy becomes "paid up," meaning the policyholder has paid as much as is required, or there is enough money built up in the cash account so that the dividends cover the premiums.

One variation on permanent life insurance that you should know about is variable life insurance. Just as with a standard permanent life policy, you pay a fixed premium amount for a variable life insurance policy. The variable part has to do with how the cash account is invested. Whereas the insurance company issuing a standard permanent life policy invests the cash value of the policy on your behalf, usually conservatively, with variable life you choose how the money is invested. You assume more risk, but you gain the potential to generate better returns.

Where Should We Buy It?

To find a good life insurance agent, ask friends for referrals. Also, my website lists some sites where you can shop for the best prices among the best companies for term insurance.

Whether you are going with a term or permanent life insurance policy, see if a credit union or any associations you belong to offer life insurance and at what price.

Be sure to check the ratings of any life insurance company you're considering. A high rating will help ensure that the life insurance company is still around if and when you need it. Two ratings organizations that offer free online information are A.M. Best Company (www.ambest.com) and Standard & Poor's (www.standardandpoors.com).

Final Life Insurance Considerations

See if the policy you are considering offers a waiver of premium rider. While it costs a little more, this rider will keep your policy in force but waive the premium if you become disabled.

Lastly, you will need to qualify medically for life insurance, which means providing information about your medical history. Most companies will send someone to your home to take blood and urine samples.

DISABILITY INSURANCE

Your ability to earn income is one of your most valuable assets. According to the nonprofit Life and Health Insurance Foundation for Education, one in seven workers can expect to be disabled for five or more years before retirement.[2] That's why disability insurance is so important, yet less than half of employed adults have disability insurance.[3]

If you are eligible for disability insurance at your place of work, you will probably find that's the least expensive place to purchase it. Should you become disabled, workplace policies typically replace 50 to 60 percent of your income up to a specified limit and until a certain age.

It is not a great idea to count on Social Security to provide for your needs if you became disabled. While you may be eligible for benefits, it can take more than a year for your claim to be processed,[4] and more than 80 percent of applicants are turned down the first time they apply.[5]

You may also be covered under worker's compensation, but this applies only if you are hurt on the job. Benefits are typically low relative to your salary and last only a few years.

If you don't have disability coverage through your employer, purchase a policy on your own. Even if your employer does offer coverage, you may want to get an individual policy if any of the following are true of your situation:

- Your employer's plan pays less than 60 percent of your salary. In this case, you may be able to buy a policy that covers another 20 percent of your income.
- Your employer's plan doesn't pay benefits to age sixty-five.
- You don't have enough savings to cover your needs until your workplace policy's waiting period is over.

You'll find more information about disability insurance, including a needs calculator, at www.lifehappens.org.

MEDICAL/DENTAL INSURANCE

If you are both employed, see whose insurance plan offers the best coverage for the price. Talk with your HR department, or if you have private health insurance, call the company directly. If one or both of you take prescription medicine, be sure to compare each policy's coverage for that benefit. This is an area where policies can vary quite a bit.

One way to save on health insurance is to opt for your company's flexible spending account (FSA), if available. With such accounts, you pay various out-of-pocket medical expenses with pretax dollars. Many expenses qualify, including co-pays, deductibles, and prescription eyeglasses. But flexible spending account money not used by the end of the year is lost (at some companies there is a short grace period into the next year), so you need to make an accurate estimate about how much out-of-pocket expenses you're likely to have over the coming year.

Another option may be a health savings account (HSA). Used in conjunction with a high-deductible health insurance plan, this money is saved pretax, just like FSA money. However, this money can be carried over from year to year and you can set aside more money in an HSA than you can an FSA. (See my website, www.MattAboutMoney .com, for the current limits and qualifying medical expenses for HSAs and FSAs.) The money carried over can also be considered another form of tax-advantaged retirement savings.

HOMEOWNERS/RENTERS INSURANCE

If you are newly married, contact the agent who handles your homeowners or renters insurance policy and make sure you have appropriate coverage for your possessions because you probably now have a lot more stuff. Also, look into riders for jewelry, such as an engagement ring and wedding rings. And make sure both of your names are on the policy.

If you own your own home, double-check the following. Some of these questions can be checked on your own; others should be discussed with your agent.

- **Is our home properly valued**? For about $8, you can estimate the replacement cost of your home at www.accucoverage.com.
- **Do we have inflation guard**? This adjusts the value of your home as the cost of building materials rise.
- **Do we have building ordinance or law coverage**? This covers any added costs of rebuilding associated with new building codes.
- **How much living expense coverage do we have**? Find out how long your policy will pay your living expenses if damage to your home would leave you living elsewhere while repairs are made.
- **Are we covered in case of a flood or sewage backup**? Even if you don't live in a flood zone, such coverage may be a good idea because you're a lot more likely to experience a flood than a fire. There is a government-run website, www.floodsmart. gov, that lets you search by address to determine your home's flood risk (look for the "One-Step Flood Risk Profile").

  As for sewer backups, most homeowners policies don't automatically cover them. A rider usually can be added for about $50 per year for $5,000 worth of coverage.

  When I called our agent, I found out that our sewage backup insurance totaled $2,500 and did not cover furniture (we upped our coverage). When I inquired about flood insurance, I was encouraged to weigh the cost (about $400 per year) against the likelihood of a flood in our area. Because the nearest river is about four miles away, its banks are much higher than the water, and the floodsmart.gov website assessed our risk as "moderate to low," we're going without the coverage.
- **Are we covered for the replacement cost of our possessions**? This covers the full value of what it would cost to replace your possessions, as opposed to cash value, which factors in depreciation.
- **Do we even know what we've got**? If you lost all that you own, would you know what you lost? Creating a detailed inventory of your stuff may not sound like your idea of a fun

Saturday afternoon project. However, should you ever lose your stuff in a fire or other disaster, you'll be glad to have done the job. The Insurance Information Institute offers an excellent free software program called Know Your Stuff (www .knowyourstuff.org) that can help with this process.

Once you've created your home inventory, e-mail a copy of it to a friend or family member so there'll be a record in case your computer is stolen or destroyed. Or save a copy on a CD or flash drive, and keep it in a safe-deposit box.

It's a good idea to use a video camera to create a visual record of what you own as well. Just walk through your house or apartment capturing all of your stuff and describing it along with your estimated value as you go. Be sure to update your inventory at least every five years.

One final type of insurance to review is vehicle insurance.

VEHICLE INSURANCE

If you have two vehicles and two different insurance policies, check with both companies to see which one offers the best price for insuring both of your vehicles. In many cases, because of multi-vehicle discounts, covering two vehicles through one company will be less expensive than the total of what you are both paying individually. You may be eligible for an additional discount if you insure your vehicles with the same company that provides your homeowners or renters insurance.

Once you combine policies, make sure both of your names are on the policy or policies.

WHERE TO FIND THE MONEY

If you are to do all that we've been discussing so far in part 2—give generously, save adequately, speed the process of getting out of debt, manage your credit score, invest a portion of all you make, and build strong walls of protection—you will need to be intentional about spending wisely on everything from groceries to gifts. In the next two chapters, we'll look at some practical ideas for doing just that.

TAKE ACTION

What to Do

Fill in the "Goal" column of the "Health" section on the *Cash Flow Plan* on page 64. If you are engaged, get an estimate of what your new medical, dental, and disability insurance policies will cost as well as an estimate for out-of-pocket prescription drug expenses, co-pays, and how much you may set aside for a health savings or flexible spending account. Then determine whether you will get life insurance policies and, if so, get a quote for the cost.

What to Discuss

- If you don't have kids, for what reasons might you consider purchasing life insurance now?
- When you purchase life insurance, are you more likely to go with a term or permanent life insurance policy? Why?
- If one of you will not be in the paid workforce, either right away or when you have kids, will you carry life insurance on that person? Why or why not?
- If you are both employed, check on the cost of adding the other to your workplace health insurance policy. How do the benefits and costs compare? Which plan do you think you will utilize?
- What other insurance-related changes will you need to make? Think about your disability, vehicle, and homeowners or renters policies.

CHAPTER 13

SPEND SMART ON HOUSING

Finish your outdoor work and get your fields ready; after that, build your house.

PROVERBS 24:27

The fellow that owns his own home is always just coming out of a hardware store.

KIN HUBBARD

ONE OF THE MOST widely held financial myths is that mortgage debt is inherently good debt. There is nothing good about taking on too large a mortgage. Spend too much on a house and it will own you. Spend the right amount and you will have great financial freedom. In this chapter, you'll find help for getting your most important spending decision right: how much to spend on where you live.

TO BUY OR NOT TO BUY?

Jude and I rented an apartment for our first ten months of marriage. Then we bought a condominium, where we lived for five years. Then

<141>

we bought a house, which is where we live now. That progression—
from renters to condo owners to homeowners—served us well. As
renters, when something breaks you call the landlord. As condo owners, when *some* things break you call the condo owner's association. As
homeowners, when anything breaks you're on your own.

It helped us on several levels to ease into the responsibility of home
ownership. Renting for those first months of our marriage gave us a
carefree way to enjoy the newness of married life. When we decided to
buy, opting for a condo introduced us to many of the responsibilities of
home ownership, but not all of the financial responsibilities. Our condo
was in a renovated old six-flat in Chicago. We had two levels of living
space: a main floor and a basement. Every time it rained heavily, we got
water in the basement, so the condo association paid for some expensive repairs to the foundation. We had to pay our share, but it was split
among the six owners. If we'd had to pay for all of the repairs on our
own, it would have hindered our financial freedom. When we finally
decided to buy a house, having owned a condo helped us prepare—financially and emotionally—to take full responsibility. If you
are engaged and neither of you owns your own home, you may want to
do something similar.

When deciding whether to buy, consider how long you will likely
stay in the home. I recommend that you don't buy the home unless you
plan on staying in it for at least five years. It typically takes that long for
your home to rise far enough in value to make back your selling costs.
Of course, this is just a guideline; as we have seen in recent history,
homes do not always go up in value.

CAN YOU AFFORD TO BUY?

When you start thinking about buying a home—whether a condo,
townhome, or single-family home—you'll need to take into account
your two main expenses: the down payment and the monthly payment.

The down payment. Ideally, I like to see people make a down payment of at least 20 percent of the purchase price. That demonstrates the discipline to save. Plus, it's the minimum threshold for not having to pay for private mortgage insurance.

Do not use emergency fund money for your down payment. A house has lots of expensive things that can go wrong. We've been in ours for only five years, yet in that time we had to have our garage torn down and rebuilt. We've also had to replace the roof of the house, the hot water heater, furnace, and air conditioner. We knew about some of these needs before we decided to buy, but not all of them.

The monthly payment. Mortgage lenders use two ratios in determining how much of a mortgage you can afford. The first one compares the combination of your monthly mortgage payment (principal and interest), property taxes, and homeowners insurance (PITI) with your income. Typically, lenders want PITI to take up no more than 28 percent of your monthly gross income. The second ratio adds in all of your other debts as well, such as any credit card balances you carry from month to month, vehicle loans, and student loans. Usually, a lender wants your housing costs plus these other debts to require no more than 40 percent of your monthly gross income. However, I strongly encourage you to aim lower.

The most you should devote to your mortgage, real estate taxes, and insurance is 25 percent of your monthly gross income — preferably less — and you should have no other debts. If you do this and follow the recommended-spending plans you'll see in Appendix A, you'll be able to give generously, save and invest adequately, and live with financial freedom.

If you are planning to buy a condominium or townhome, include at least part of your monthly homeowners association fee (also known as your "assessment") in the 25 percent. Part of it can also be considered home maintenance.

In high-real-estate-cost areas such as California and parts of the East Coast, you might need to devote 30 percent of your monthly gross income to housing. Of course, that means you'll have to spend less on other categories. (In Appendix B, you'll see more detailed income-based recommendations for how much to spend on a house.)

If you are renting, keep the combination of your rent, renters insurance, and utilities to no more than 25 percent of your monthly gross income. I include utilities for the rent calculation because renters don't pay real estate taxes. Doing so should also give you an added buffer between your income and expenses, which will help you save for a down payment if you plan to buy a home.

....

Don't Succumb to Delusions of DINKhood

If marriage will turn you into a double-income-no-kids (DINK) household, it'll be tempting to live it up. Just think of the house you'll be able to afford, the cars, and the nights on the town! But hold on a minute. Before you start dreaming of movin' on up to the good part of town, consider this: Do you want to have children someday? If so, would you want the financial flexibility to be able to choose to have one of you stay home? Making sure your monthly housing costs (mortgage principal and interest, real estate taxes, and homeowners insurance) require no more than 25 percent of one income will be the single biggest factor that will enable you to do that.

Even if you don't plan to have kids, it's wise to make sure you base your housing costs on one income. Otherwise, what if one of you lost your job? How would you pay the mortgage?

I once talked with a husband and wife who had succumbed to the delusions of DINKhood: two leased cars, frequent dinners out, and a mortgage that required a large portion of their combined high incomes. Then the woman lost her job. When they talked to me, their faces were full of fear. His had a tinge of anger. How could she lose her job and put their lives in such peril? But it wasn't her fault. They had both chosen that high-risk path.

My advice is to build your lifestyle primarily on one income. Of course, base your generosity on both incomes. If you have debt, use the second income to wipe it out. Next, boost your savings and investments. If kids are in your future and one of you wants to stay home, investing a good portion of that second income now will help make it possible to invest sufficiently on just one income down the road. Then, sure, enjoy a portion of that second income. By following this advice, Jude and I were able to take four overseas vacations before our first child was born.

CHOOSING A MORTGAGE

There are different types of mortgages and different ways that mortgage interest rates are set. Let's look at these differences so that you can choose the right mortgage at the best price.

Mortgage types. There are two major types of mortgages: an FHA mortgage, which is guaranteed by the Federal Housing Authority, and a conventional mortgage, which requires adherence to the more stringent underwriting requirements set by Fannie Mae and Freddie Mac.

The down payment required for an FHA mortgage is just 3.5 percent of the purchase price. That money can be a gift from your parents or someone else. You may even qualify with a relatively low credit score, such as one in the upper 600s. However, because the FHA provides mortgages for people with less than stellar credit, two layers of mortgage insurance are required. First, there is an upfront insurance premium equal to a percentage of the mortgage. As I was writing this book it was 2.25 percent. Take out a loan for $100,000, for example, and you will actually be borrowing $102,250. Then you'll pay an additional monthly mortgage insurance premium. Because of these added costs, I recommend waiting until you can afford and qualify for a conventional mortgage.

To obtain a conventional mortgage, you'll need a credit score in the mid 700s. The rules allow for a minimum down payment of 5 percent, which must be your own funds. No gifts allowed. If you put down more than 5 percent, the additional amount can be from gifts.

With a conventional mortgage, there is no upfront mortgage insurance. However, if you put less than 20 percent down, you will pay a monthly mortgage insurance premium. The amount of that premium drops a lot if you can afford to put 10 percent down as opposed to 5 percent.

Despite the rules allowing you to obtain a conventional mortgage with less than 20 percent down, I still recommend waiting until you can afford to make a 20 percent down payment.

Interest rate terms. In general, there are two ways that mortgage interest rates are set. In fixed-rate mortgages, the interest rate remains the same for the life of the mortgage, typically fifteen or thirty years. In adjustable-rate mortgages (ARM), the interest rate may be fixed for anywhere from one to ten years. Then it adjusts based on various indices.

I recommend that you choose a fixed-rate mortgage. Countless people have gotten themselves in trouble with adjustable-rate mortgages. They assumed they would sell their home before their rate adjusted, only to find out for a variety of reasons they needed to stay longer. Or they assumed they would refinance into a fixed-rate mortgage, only to find out they didn't qualify because their home decreased in value or their income dropped.

A fifteen-year fixed-rate mortgage will cost more per month than a thirty-year mortgage, but you will pay far less in interest over the life of the loan. If you opt for a thirty-year mortgage, make sure there are no prepayment penalties. Going that route will give you a more affordable monthly payment and also the flexibility to pay more in order to speed the process of paying off the mortgage while reducing your overall interest costs. If you make extra payments, it is usually best to write a separate check and note that it is for principal only. Check with the company servicing your mortgage to make sure you are following their procedures for making extra principal payments.

Shopping for a mortgage. Once you know what type of mortgage you are looking for and the interest rate terms, get quotes from at least three direct mortgage lenders or mortgage brokers. Banks and credit unions are examples of direct mortgage lenders. Mortgage brokers have relationships with multiple direct lenders.

Ask each one for an estimate of their total fees. They will have their own fees (lender fees), third-party fees (appraisal, credit report, title search, and other fees), and various "point" payment options. A point is an up-front fee that buys you a lower interest rate. Ask each one for the same set of options: their interest rate for a no-point loan along with their fees and an estimate of all third-party fees, as well as their interest rates if you were to pay down the rate through various point payment options. Try to get all quotes on the same day. Because rates change so often, that will give you a true comparison and enable you to choose the lender or broker who charges the least amount in fees for the same interest rate loan.

THE ROLE OF CREDIT SCORES

Your credit scores will play a significant role in determining whether you will qualify for a mortgage and, if so, at what interest rate. On the next page is an example of how different credit scores impact what you would pay for a $250,000 mortgage:[1]

Before you apply for a mortgage, it's a good idea to get your credit score. As I mentioned in chapter 2, you can buy your FICO credit score at www.myfico.com for $15.95. If you are just learning about credit scores for the first time, getting your score from one credit bureau is fine. However, when you decide to buy a home, buy both of the FICO scores that are available to you, the one from TransUnion and the one from Equifax.

FICO Chart

FICO Score	Interest Rate	Monthly Payment
760–850	4.485%	$1,264
700–759	4.707%	$1,298
680–699	4.884%	$1,324
660–679	5.098%	$1,357
640–659	5.528%	$1,424
620–639	6.074%	$1,511

Your two FICO scores should be similar to each other, within about fifty points. If they differ more than that, something may have been misreported to one of the credit bureaus, so go over your credit reports with a fine-tooth comb (see chapter 10 for more about how to do this).

If you and your spouse are applying for a mortgage jointly, both of your credit scores will be taken into account. I should say all six of your credit scores, because each of you has three scores, one from each of the three major credit bureaus. Lenders typically base their decision of whether to offer you a loan, and at what rate, on the lower of both of your middle scores.

If you are following my advice and applying for a mortgage that will require only one income and the person whose income you will use has a credit score in the mid-700s or higher, you don't need to worry about the other person's score, at least not for the purpose of applying for your mortgage. It is fine to apply for the mortgage in only one person's name. However, as long as both of you have strong credit scores, you may still want to apply in both of your names. That way, the mortgage will show up on both of your credit reports, and having a mortgage on your report may further strengthen your score, assuming of course that you make your payments on time.

Rapid Rescoring

If you have reason to believe that you could improve your credit score, either by paying down a debt or fixing a mistake on your credit report, and if you can't wait thirty days to see if your score will in fact improve, see if your mortgage broker works with a rapid rescoring service. For a fee, such services may be able to get the credit bureaus to update your credit report within days, which will change your credit score. But they can help only if you find a legitimate problem and the creditor involved has acknowledged they made a mistake or if you have taken meaningful action, such as paying down a large portion of your debt.

In chapter 10, I mentioned that applying for lots of new credit in a short amount of time could hurt your credit score. When a prospective lender checks your credit report, that's known as a "hard inquiry," and you don't want lots of hard inquiries within a short period of time. However, you generally do not need to worry about this when applying for a mortgage from multiple lenders. Usually, multiple mortgage inquiries within a short period of time count as only one inquiry.[2]

SMALLER EXPENSES MATTER TOO

If you want to enjoy financial peace of mind, the best thing you can do is keep your housing costs manageable. Of course, there are many other spending categories to manage as well. In the next chapter, we'll review the remaining categories listed on the *Cash Flow Plan* in order, highlighting many ways to spend smart.

TAKE ACTION

What to Do

Fill in the "Goal" column of the "Housing" category on your *Cash Flow Plan* on page 64. Do you know where you will live? If so, you should be able to enter the mortgage or rent cost and, if applicable, the monthly cost for real estate taxes. Then decide which company you will use for renters or homeowners insurance and get a quote.

What to Discuss

- If you do not own a home right now, how has this chapter impacted your thinking about:
  - When to buy a home?
  - How much to put down?
  - Whether to base your monthly housing payments on one income or two?
  - What type of mortgage to obtain (FHA or conventional? Fixed or adjustable-rate?)
- If you already own a home that requires both of your incomes, would you consider selling the home in order to purchase one you can afford on one income?

CHAPTER 14

SPEND SMART ON ALL OTHER EXPENSES

If you have not been trustworthy in handling worldly wealth,
who will trust you with true riches?

LUKE 16:11

Economy is half the battle of life; it is not so hard to earn money
as to spend it well.

C. H. SPURGEON

SPENDING SMART IS NOT about obsessive frugality; it's about being proactive, learning quick and simple steps that will help you get discounts, and cultivating the mindset of a smart shopper. Every spending category presents opportunities to spend wisely, and doing so frees up money for the things that matter most. We covered your largest expense category in the last chapter. Now here are my favorite ways to spend smart in each of the remaining categories on the *Cash Flow Plan.*

<151>

MAINTENANCE/UTILITIES

Homes need constant tending. The paint needs touching up, furnace filters need replacing, bricks need tuck-pointing, and appliances need to be repaired or replaced. Learn to do some projects yourself and you will save money. Then again, taking on projects that are over your head can end up costing you more, so know your limits. On the websites of the national home improvement stores, you will find free guides, some with instructional videos, walking you through numerous do-it-yourself projects. Check my website, www.MattAboutMoney.com, for the latest links.

You can save on the cost of utilities by switching from regular lightbulbs to compact fluorescent lightbulbs. CFLs, as they're known, cost a little bit more, but they use just 25 percent of the energy of conventional lightbulbs and last much longer. The only caution is that CFLs contain a small amount of mercury. If you break one, you have to be careful about how you clean up the mess. When one burns out, do not put the bulb in your regular garbage; take it to a hazardous waste disposal facility. Some retail stores are also drop-off sites for CFLs, including Home Depot, Lowe's, and IKEA. For more on how to clean up a broken CFL and where to find a disposal facility, go to www.earth911.com.

Other ways to save on the cost of utilities include the following:

- Use a programmable thermostat to control your home's temperature, setting it to automatically switch to a more cost-effective temperature at nighttime or while you are both away.
- Drop your landline and use just your cell phones.
- Now here's a crazy-sounding idea: Go without an Internet connection at home. I know, that sounds impossible, right? But if you are trying to get out of debt or build savings, going without an Internet connection for the next six to twelve months may help put you on the fast track toward the accomplishment of those goals.

TRANSPORTATION

You'll notice that I do not include a line for vehicle payments in this category. That's because such payments are debt payments, and I recommend you commit to paying cash for vehicles. Here's how to do so.

First, once your car is paid off, keep making the payments. Just send them to a savings account instead of the finance company. Second, keep your vehicles a long time. If you keep up with the basic maintenance, most cars will be reliable for at least ten years and often much longer. Third, when you're ready to buy, consult *Consumer Reports* for their recommendations on the most reliable cars in your price range. Also, use the True Cost to Own tool at www.edmunds.com to compare the ongoing costs of each vehicle you are considering, including maintenance, insurance, fuel, and more.

I don't recommend leasing vehicles because doing so creates an ongoing expense. You will come out ahead if you purchase well-cared-for used cars with cash and keep them for a long time.

Once you have a sufficient emergency fund, raise your collision and comprehensive deductibles on your vehicle insurance policy. Talk to your insurance agent to see how much less you will pay for different deductibles. Just keep in mind, you are now self-insuring for those amounts.

Be sure to budget for vehicle maintenance and repairs. The amount depends on the age and condition of your vehicle, but a good ballpark is $75 per month per vehicle.

You can also save money on transportation by using your vehicles less often. Commuting to work with a coworker or friend who lives and works near where you live and work, even one day a week, will save on your fuel and maintenance costs. See if you can walk or ride your bike to places where you would normally drive.

If you have two vehicles, consider whether you need both. If one of you could take public transportation to work, you may be able to get by just fine with one vehicle and you'll save a lot on insurance, maintenance, and other costs. We went from two vehicles to one a couple of years ago and have never regretted the decision. When we absolutely need a second vehicle, we rent one.

TAXES

Pay your taxes on time, but don't overpay. More than 70 percent of taxpayers get a refund each year, and the average amount is more than $2,500. That's a significant overpayment of taxes.

You can estimate how much you are likely to pay in taxes once you are married by going to www.irs.gov, searching for "Withholding calculator," and then estimating how much you should be paying in federal taxes. It's fine to get a small refund each year, but if it looks as though you'll get back more than $500, talk with someone in your employer's human resources department about having less money withheld from your paycheck.

FOOD

Just following some commonsense ideas will help you spend effectively in this category. Each weekend, plan ahead for what you'll make for dinner over the next week. Then make your grocery list before going to the store, and try different stores to see which ones have the best prices for the items you buy most often. Jude and I have one store where we do most of our food shopping. But we also buy certain items at Target and at the deep discounter Aldi.

Check out the many great coupon websites online. They make it relatively easy to find coupons for items that are also on sale at stores near you. Some of my favorites are listed on my website. If you buy organic foods, check my website for a helpful guide from *Consumer Reports* that recommends which foods are worth paying more for in order to get the organic versions and which ones are not worth the added cost.

CLOTHING

Many discount clothing stores offer great prices on brand-name cloth-ing. Also try secondhand stores. Jude will often stop at the Goodwill store close to our pediatrician's office. She regularly finds great deals there, especially on clothes for our kids. Some of the clothing is even brand-new, as several department stores drop off unsold items.

In addition, "shop" your closet. I have heard that the average person regularly wears only 20 percent of the clothing in his or her closet. That sounds about right. So the next time you feel that you need something new, take a look inside your closet. Chances are you will find some-thing you haven't worn in a while that still fits and looks good.

Clothing swaps have also become popular. These are events where everyone brings items he or she no longer wants and then swaps them for other items free of charge. Consider organizing one at your church or where you work.

Lastly, buy clothing that does not require dry cleaning.

HOUSEHOLD/PERSONAL

One of the most important categories here is gifts. Because gift giving tends to ebb and flow throughout the year, make a list of all the people you plan to buy gifts for this year (you'll find a form on my website that helps make this easy). Then set an annual gift budget, divide by twelve, and put that amount into your savings account for periodic bills and expenses each month. You'll find this especially helpful at Christmastime, because that's when a lot of people who did not plan ahead end up going into debt buying Christmas presents.

For furniture, shop garage sales, estate sales, and secondhand stores. We still use a patio table and chairs Jude bought at a thrift store before we met.

ENTERTAINMENT

Cable or satellite television is not a utility expense; it is entertainment. Consider lower-cost packages or going without such services. If you have an older television, you can buy a digital signal converter box at an electronics store, or if you have a newer television, it should be able to pick up the free digital signals from nearby television stations. Today, many programs are available at no or low cost through the Internet. See my website for recommended sites.

When going out to eat, see if a discount coupon is available. The website www.restaurant.com regularly offers $25 certificates for specific restaurants for $10, but the discounts run even deeper than that. If you give them your e-mail address, you will often receive coupon codes where you can purchase $25 certificates for just $2. There are usually restrictions as to what nights the discounts are available and certain minimum-purchase requirements, but if you're going out to eat anyway, you might as well see if a discount certificate is available.

When was the last time you visited your local library? Besides books, libraries have movies on DVD, music CDs, computers with Internet access, and sometimes even free tickets to museums, zoos, or music venues near you. If you subscribe to a DVD service, you might consider dropping that in favor of getting free DVDs at your library.

ADDITIONAL CATEGORIES

Here are some other categories and ideas for how to spend smart:

Health. As mentioned in chapter 12, make use of flexible spending or health savings accounts. Also, at the risk of sounding parental, take care of yourself. Just going for walks on a regular basis will help save on the cost of healthcare.

Child care. If and when you have kids, you'll find that babysitting can easily become a big expense. Trade babysitting duties with your friends who also have kids. You sit for their kids once a month; they sit for yours once a month.

Miscellaneous. Everyone incurs expenses that defy definition, so budget at least $50 per month for miscellaneous expenses.

Use the Internet to Score Multiple Discounts. When shopping for something that is sold in more than one store, use a comparison-shopping website to see who has the best price. You'll find a list of my favorite sites on my website (go to www.MattAboutMoney.com and click on "Resources").

For everything from rental cars to electronics, you should be able to double-dip on discounts; sometimes you can even triple-dip. I'm in the habit of first looking for a discount code at www.retailmenot.com and then going to www.ebates.com and entering the retailer's website from there. By using both, I get a discount on the purchase and also a little money back in the form of a rebate check. I did that when renting a car recently and also used a coupon from the Entertainment Book we bought from our four-year-old's preschool. A discount is a good thing; three discounts are even better.

I also triple-dipped when buying tires for our vehicle. I researched the type of tires I wanted to buy, discovered that Sears was offering a $70 rebate, found an additional $5-off coupon code online, and then made the purchase online (while setting up an appointment for installation) after entering the Sears site through Ebates, which generated an additional $20 rebate.

THE SAVINGS WILL ADD UP

Start putting the ideas in this chapter into action and you'll improve the effectiveness of your spending in every category. Remember, these suggestions are not about obsessive frugality; they're about spending smart so you have more money for what matters most. For a steady stream of new ideas about spending wisely, subscribe to my blog at www.MattAboutMoney.com.

TAKE ACTION

What to Do

On page 64, finish your *Cash Flow Plan* goals, making sure your budget balances. Income minus outgo should equal zero. Use the recommended-spending plans in Appendix A to get some ideas for appropriate amounts to spend in each category. You don't have to follow the recommendations exactly. Maybe you value vacations more than new clothing. The benchmarks should help you see if you are wildly off in your assumptions in some categories.

What to Discuss

- What are some of your favorite money-saving ideas that were not listed in this chapter?
- Will you each bring a vehicle into your marriage? How well could you manage with just one?
- Are you in the habit of buying groceries or clothing at only certain stores? What other stores might you try? Have you been to a secondhand store recently? If so, what did you find there?
- Will you subscribe to cable or satellite television when you get married? Could you go without it?
- How large an income tax refund do you usually receive? What do you usually do with your refund? Would you be better off having less money taken out of your paychecks?

PART THREE

FOSTERING FINANCIAL ONENESS

CHAPTER 15

ONE IN LOVE,
ONE IN MONEY

A man will leave his father and mother and be united with his wife, and they will become one flesh.

GENESIS 2:24

We have the greatest prenuptial agreement in the world. It's called love.

GENE PERRET

YOU ARE IN THE midst of one of the happiest phases of life, but it can also be stressful. If you are engaged, there are countless decisions to be made about your wedding. If you are newly married, there's a lot to be done in bringing your lives together, financially and otherwise. This chapter is designed to guide you through the three key businesslike details of marriage: determining whether a prenuptial agreement is right for you, setting up your checking and savings accounts, and figuring out what to do with your credit cards.

<161>

WHAT'S UP WITH PRENUPS?

One of the hottest topics on the marriage circuit today is whether you should have a prenuptial agreement ("prenup"). While only 3 percent of married or engaged people have a prenup, fully one-third of single people say they would ask their spouse-to-be to sign one,[1] and 40 percent of divorced people say they would do so if they remarried.

A prenuptial agreement is a legal document negotiated before you marry that specifies how you will divide up your assets if your marriage doesn't work out. A prenup can also help direct what happens to the assets of one spouse upon his or her death. Each party uses his or her own attorney to review the document before signing.

Some secular personal finance writers and estate planning attorneys believe that every couple should have a prenup. They point out that half of all marriages end in divorce, so why risk adding financial pain to the emotional pain of a breakup? On the other hand, some Christian personal finance writers and estate planning attorneys believe that no one should have a prenup. They point out that marriage is a sacred covenant and a relationship that is intended to last "until death do us part." They believe that a prenuptial agreement undermines a couple's marriage and may even increase the likelihood of divorce.

Prenups are typically recommended for two reasons:

1. Wealth protection. When one person is bringing a lot of wealth into the marriage and the other person is not, or when one stands to receive a sizeable inheritance, those in the pro-prenup camp say a prenup makes sense. I disagree.

Marriage should be entered into with the goal of oneness in all things, including finances. If one person was wealthy before getting married, that person's wealth becomes the couple's joint wealth from their wedding day forward. If you fear that marriage will put your wealth at risk, perhaps your money means more to you than your future spouse does. I encourage you to hold off on your wedding until you resolve that.

2. Other person protection. There are situations where the breakup of your marriage may hurt other people financially. Prenup advocates say this is another scenario where a prenup is called for. Here they may have a valid point.

Imagine this: One spouse—let's say the man—has children from a previous marriage. In order to make sure those children receive an inheritance, he could put certain assets into a revocable living trust and also use a prenup in which his new wife waives any interest in those assets should he die. Using a revocable trust allows him the flexibility to make changes. Perhaps when his children become adults, he will decide that his wife would benefit more than his adult children from some or all of the assets in the trust. But if he sets up a trust without a prenup, here's a potential problem: Upon his death, his wife could attempt to claim a share of the trust assets using a process known as elective share, in which she would give up what she was entitled to as specified in his will and, depending on state law, demand up to 50 percent of his entire estate instead. However, a prenup trumps elective share. It would add a layer of protection for the children, further ensuring they will receive what their father intended for them to receive.

Still, even if you believe that a prenup would make sense for your situation, there may be alternatives. Because some people cringe at the thought of using a prenup, it's worth exploring the options. Here's a real-life situation similar to the one we just looked at where an alternative tool accomplished the same result. Joe's second wife did not get along with his children. When Joe died suddenly in a car accident, the children from his first marriage received an inheritance because he had set up irrevocable life insurance trusts for them. This was an ironclad way of providing an inheritance to those children without subjecting them to any negotiations with their stepmother.

Here are the main questions to consider regarding the use of a prenuptial agreement:

- If I am the one recommending the use of a prenup, am I overly concerned about protecting wealth I am bringing into the marriage?
- If my fiancé/fiancée is asking for a prenup, is that conveying a lack of trust in me? Am I comfortable with the request?
- Would anyone other than my spouse or me suffer financially if our marriage fails? If so, are there other ways we could protect that person besides a prenup? (Talk with a Christian estate planning attorney about this.) If there are no viable alternatives, are we both in agreement about the use of a prenup?

In an ideal world, there would be no divorce and hence no need for prenuptial agreements. But we do not live in an ideal world. Still, before pushing for a prenup, pray that God would search your heart and check your motives. Consider other alternatives first, and whatever you decide, make sure there is unity in the decision with your future spouse.

MERGE YOUR CHECKING AND SAVINGS ACCOUNTS

When marriage blogger Dustin Riechmann (www.engagedmarriage .com) wrote an article advocating the use of joint checking accounts in marriage, he was surprised at the reaction. "My wife and I have always had a joint checking account. I thought that's what happily married couples do." The article generated an outpouring of reader comments, with strong opinions on both sides.

Those in favor of separate checking and savings accounts said it works best to divvy up the financial responsibilities: "You pay the mortgage, I'll cover the groceries and utilities." Those who supported joint accounts argued that marriage is about oneness and having joint accounts fosters oneness. I'm in the joint account camp.

As we saw in chapter 1, there can be a lot of financial secret keeping in marriage, which is not good for your finances or your relationship.

Using joint accounts provides financial transparency and fosters team-work. Some say a joint account hinders each person's freedom, but that doesn't need to be the case. I recommend that each spouse have his or her own budgeted amounts to spend as he or she pleases. Doing so doesn't require separate accounts.

When I discuss this in my workshops, I am often asked how it's possible to surprise each other with presents if a couple has joint bank accounts. There are a couple of ways to do this. First, have three gift budgets: one for gifts you buy for your spouse, one for gifts he or she buys for you, and one for gifts you buy as a couple for other people. In order to make a gift a surprise, withdraw your budgeted amount from an ATM and pay for the purchase with cash. On your *Cash Flow Tracker* on page 68, indicate that the money was spent on a gift; you don't need to be specific, at least not until after you've given the gift. If using a credit card, just make the purchase close enough to the gift-giving occasion that the statement will arrive afterward so your spouse will be surprised when receiving the gift. Another option is to use your gift-budget money to buy a gift card or gift check and then use it to buy a gift for your spouse. You may have to pay a small fee, but your specific purchase won't show up on a credit card statement.

Once you've set up your bank or credit union accounts as husband and wife, you need to choose a form of ownership. The most common one among married couples is known as "joint ownership with rights of survivorship," or in community property states, "community property with rights of survivorship." With such accounts, when one owner dies, the other owns the account outright. You should also name beneficiaries.

How will combining checking and savings accounts impact the insurance provided by your bank or credit union for your checking and savings accounts? In short, this is not likely to be an issue. For one thing, the insurance limits are high; most people don't have that much money on deposit with a bank or credit union. For another thing, Federal Deposit Insurance Corporation (FDIC) insurance and the most common form of credit union insurance limits are doubled for joint accounts.

FDIC insurance limits are $250,000 per depositor per insured bank, which includes the total that you have in checking, savings, money market accounts, and certificates of deposit. If you each had $250,000 in an FDIC-insured bank before getting married, those amounts would have been fully insured. After you get married, if you set up your accounts as jointly owned, your combined $500,000 will still be fully insured because the insurance limit of $250,000 pertains to each depositor, making the limit $500,000 for accounts that are co-owned. You can get more information about FDIC insurance at www.fdic.gov.

If you have money in a credit union, make sure it is insured by the National Credit Union Share Insurance Fund (NCUSIF), which is a fund backed by the full faith and credit of the United States government, or American Share Insurance (ASI), which is private credit union insurance. NCUSIF insurance limits are the same as those of the FDIC: up to $250,000 held by an individual across checking, savings, or money market accounts or CDs. A joint account is insured up to $500,000. For more information, start at the National Credit Union Association website at www.ncua.gov.

ASI provides more generous coverage for individual credit union members than the NCUSIF in that it covers up to $250,000 for *each account* held by an ASI-insured credit union member rather than the member's combined holdings. Jointly held accounts are also insured up to $250,000, which sounds less favorable. However, if you had more than that on deposit, you could always open multiple joint accounts. There's more information at www.americanshare.com.

DECIDE WHAT TO DO ABOUT YOUR CREDIT CARDS

The first step in dealing with your credit cards after getting married is to call the companies that issued your credit cards and let them know about any change to your name or address. They will begin reporting your new name to the credit bureaus, which means your credit reports will start showing both your old name and your new name. This should not impact your credit history.

The next step is to decide whether to turn any of your credit card accounts into joint user accounts, adding your name to your spouse's cards and vice versa. While I generally encourage you to do all that you can to foster financial oneness in marriage, there are no major benefits to turning your credit cards into joint user accounts, and in fact there may be some drawbacks.

If either of you is bringing a high credit card balance into the marriage, it is usually best to keep that card in that person's name only. If you turn it into a joint user account, you may negatively impact the other person's credit score.

Even if neither of you has a high balance on your cards, it still may be best not to make any changes. If one of you cancels a card, that could increase your credit utilization, which could hurt your credit score. Credit utilization is the percentage of available credit you are using. If you cancel a card, you will lower your total available credit, which may increase your utilization.

Here's an example. Let's say you both have two credit cards, each of which has a $5,000 credit limit ($10,000 total credit limit), and you both typically charge a total of $2,000 per month. That's 20 percent of your available credit. Now let's assume one of you decides to cancel both of your cards in favor of becoming a joint user on your spouse's cards. If you keep charging as you usually do, both charging $2,000 per month, now both of you are using 40 percent of your available credit. Both of your credit scores are likely to suffer. So before considering whether to close any accounts and/or become joint users, consider the impact on your credit utilization.

Now, what if one of you is bringing a low credit score into the marriage? Are there ways the spouse with the good score can help the other? It depends on what is causing the one spouse's low score. If the low score was caused by negative information such as a bankruptcy, foreclosure, or history of late payments, only time will heal those wounds. But if the low score is due to high credit utilization, it may help if the spouse with the good score adds the spouse with the bad score as an authorized user on an account or two, as long as those accounts have low or no balances.

This is different than the joint user designation. The person with the good credit score does not have any of the existing debt carried by the person with the bad credit score applied to his or her credit utilization. However, the person being added as an authorized user may benefit from the arrangement. As long as the account shows up on the person's credit report, he or she will gain a higher credit limit against which his or her debts are measured for credit utilization purposes.

Of course, a better way to deal with a high utilization problem is to pay down your balances.

The single most important aspect of managing credit cards successfully as husband and wife is making sure both of your credit card purchases feed into a central cash-flow-tracking system. That way, even though you might be using cards held in your individual names, there is still complete transparency; you are both seeing what the other is charging. If you are using budget software or an online budget tool such as Mint.com, make sure all of your credit cards are tied into the system. If you are tracking purchases manually, make sure you are both sharing the details of each purchase you make using credit cards.

MORE THAN MONEY

How you manage money in your household will impact so much more than your finances. Jude often says, and I agree, that how couples manage money is a metaphor for their marriage. Strive for oneness and teamwork in your finances, and such characteristics will show up in other areas of your relationship as well.

TAKE ACTION

What to Do

If you are not married yet, review the terms of the checking and savings accounts you both use. Check on fees and minimum-balance requirements. This will help you decide whose bank or credit union to use after you are married.

What to Discuss

- Do either of you see a need for a prenup? Why or why not?
- Will you turn your checking and savings accounts into joint accounts? Why or why not?
- Whose bank or credit union will you use?
- After reading the section about credit cards, would it make sense for either of you to add the other as an authorized user on one or more accounts?

DETAILS, DETAILS

Be sure you know the condition of your flocks, give careful attention to your herds.

PROVERBS 27:23

I've actually considered going with my married name, Julia Hall, but all the paperwork.

JULIA LOUIS-DREYFUS

WHEN YOU GET ENGAGED and then marry, there are countless details that need attention. To help you remember what you need to do, I've listed in chronological and priority order the many decisions, documents, and declarations that come with the territory of getting married, along with my recommendations on how to best take care of each one. Put a check mark in the box next to each topic title after you have taken care of that detail.

☐ GET LICENSED AND CERTIFIED

If you're engaged, one of the first marriage-related documents you'll need is a marriage license, which will authorize you to get married. You will need to apply for a license in person from the state in which you

<171>

plan to marry. So if you live in Arizona but plan to marry in California, you will need a license from California. The laws governing marriage licenses vary by state, so contact the city or county clerk's office where you plan to get married. Doing an Internet search on the city and state where you plan to marry plus "marriage license" will get you to the right office that issues licenses. Timing is everything when getting a marriage license. Don't put this off too long because some states have waiting periods, but don't get your license too far in advance either as licenses are valid for only so long.

While you'll need a marriage *license* before getting married, you'll need a marriage *certificate* after you're married. This piece of paper proves you are indeed husband and wife. The person performing your wedding will sign your marriage license and then return it to the city or county clerk's office. Some clerk's offices will automatically send you your certificate. With others, you will have to request it and pay for it.

If you ever lose your marriage certificate (or birth certificate), you can purchase a new copy through the office where you got your license, at www.vitalchek.com, or through some currency exchanges.

☐ TELL YOUR EMPLOYER

After you are married, contact your employer's HR department and fill out a new W-4 form ("Employee's Withholding Allowance Certificate"), indicating your new marital status.

If you have your paycheck direct deposited, ask your employer to make sure the name on your company's records is the same as what's listed on your bank account (more on bank accounts later). Be sure they have your new name if you are changing it and that you are consistent in how you use your name (for example, "Susan" or "Sue," hyphenated or not).

☐ TELL THE SOCIAL SECURITY ADMINISTRATION

If you're changing your name, you need a new Social Security card. After you receive your marriage certificate, go to www.socialsecurity.gov, look for the "Other Useful Links" drop-down menu, and choose "Marriage, Divorce, Name Changes." Or, if the site changes by the time you read this book, just search for "Marriage and name changes" to get the instructions and forms you need to obtain a new Social Security card.

☐ POSSIBLY GET A NEW DRIVER'S LICENSE

By law, you may need to notify your Secretary of State's or Department of Motor Vehicles' office about a change of address within a short amount of time. In Illinois, for example, within ten days of changing your name or address, you need to notify the Secretary of State's office. There is no fee for making this change and it can be done online. You then have another twenty days to obtain a new driver's license. Doing so requires a visit to a driver's services facility and payment of a fee. Check your state's requirements by going to www.usa.gov and searching for "Renew your driver's license."

☐ TELL YOUR UTILITY COMPANIES

Contact all of your utility companies to ask them to update their records with both of your names. That way, either one of you can make changes to the services you receive. This includes electric, gas, water, garbage, and phone companies (landline and cell). While I don't consider cable and satellite television services to be utilities (they are entertainment), you'll want to notify them as well.

☐ UPDATE YOUR INVESTMENT ACCOUNTS

You can change taxable investment accounts from individual accounts to joint accounts, and I recommend you do so for the same reasons I mentioned regarding checking and savings accounts. If you have changed your name, you'll need to notify these companies about that. Plus, review your beneficiary designations; you will probably want to make your spouse the primary beneficiary.

The account ownership story is different for tax-advantaged accounts such as a 401(k), 403(b), or 457(b) plan or an IRA. By law, these accounts can only be individual accounts. Still, you'll need to update any name-change information and beneficiary designations.

☐ UPDATE YOUR LIFE INSURANCE BENEFICIARIES

If either of you brought life insurance into your marriage, be sure your beneficiary designations are up to date. Typically, each of you will name the other as the primary beneficiary. However, you also need secondary beneficiaries.

☐ UPDATE YOUR REAL ESTATE TITLE

If you owned property before getting married and you changed your name after getting married, you will need to update your property title or deed.

It is best to put both of your names on the title to a home owned by one spouse prior to your marriage. That way, should one of you die, the other will own the property without it having to go through probate.

Find out what the options are for titling the property jointly in your state by talking with a real estate or estate planning attorney. In some cases, your best option will be to title your property as "joint tenancy with rights of survivorship" (in community property states, the equivalent is "community property with rights of survivorship"). In the event of one spouse's death, the property transfers to the surviving spouse without going through probate. You may benefit from titling your property as "tenancy by the entirety" if the designation is available in your state. As with "joint tenancy with rights of survivorship," upon the death of one spouse, the property transfers to the other. However, one other benefit of "tenancy by the entirety" is that if one of you were sued, the lawsuit could not force the sale of the property.

While having both of your names on the title to property owned by one of you prior to marriage makes sense, both of your names do not need to be on the mortgage. Whereas the title governs ownership of the property, the mortgage dictates who's responsible for making payments. The only time you may want to add the other spouse to the mortgage would be if you decide to refinance the mortgage and that spouse's credit score enables you to qualify for a more favorable interest rate.

☐ UPDATE YOUR VEHICLE TITLE AND REGISTRATION

I recommend putting both of your names on the titles and registration cards to any vehicles you own as well. That way, if one spouse dies, the vehicle becomes the property of the surviving spouse without it having to go through probate.

You may be able to make these changes at the same time you change your driver's license. You can find out how at the same site I mentioned for getting information about changing your driver's license (go to www.usa.gov and search for "Renew your driver's license").

☐ HAVE WILLS DRAFTED

More than any other document, a will puts you in touch with your mortality. That probably explains why 65 percent of adults in the U.S. do not have a will.[1] However, if you care about what happens to your property after you die—in essence, if you care about the provision for loved ones you leave behind—you need a will.

It's true that even without a will, some assets will end up where you want them. As we've discussed, property titled in both of your names will go to the surviving spouse upon the other's death whether you have a will or not. Likewise, assets with proper beneficiary designations will go to whomever you designate. That's why it's important to update your ownership and beneficiary designations as soon as possible after you marry.

However, for everything else—property held in your name only, including a closely held business; assets without a beneficiary designated; and items without the option of specifying the owner or beneficiary (artwork, jewelry, coin collections, your grand champion Chihuahua)—if you die without a will, your state's intestate laws will determine who gets what.

While such laws vary from state to state, in most cases (but not all), if you die without a will and have no children, your property will transfer to your spouse. That may not sound so bad, but consider this: What if you and your spouse died in the same accident and neither of you had a will? In some states, if one of you lived a bit longer than the other, the parents of the one who lived the longest would get all of your property. Would that be your preference?

Or consider this: In Illinois, if you leave behind a spouse and a child, half of your estate would go to your spouse and half to your child. If the child were a minor, a court would have the authority to name a guardian to manage that child's portion of your estate. At age eighteen or twenty-one, depending on your state, the child would receive his or her portion of the estate with no restrictions. Is that what you would want?

Your state has strict guidelines as to which relatives are entitled to your assets, and chances are good that its plan is not your intended plan. If you have the desire to leave anything to your church or other nonprofits, you don't want to choose your state's plan. You won't find any charities on its distribution list.

Typically, a married couple will opt for mirror wills. If you die, everything goes to your spouse; if he/she dies, everything goes to you.

It is all the more important for each of you to have a will once you have children, because this is the document in which you will name a legal guardian for your kids in the event of both of your deaths. The guardian may also be in charge of managing any money your children would receive upon reaching your state's age of adulthood. Or, if money management isn't the legal guardian's strength, you could name someone else or even a financial institution to handle the money-management responsibilities. In most states, you can use a will to specify when your children would receive their inheritance. Check with an estate planning attorney in your state to see if that's the case where you live. Using a will to put those restrictions in place may be less expensive than doing so in a trust.

Of course, talk to your proposed guardians before naming them in your will to make sure they are comfortable with that responsibility. Before having kids, you can save on the cost of updating your will by naming a guardian for "future children."

When you get wills drafted, get the following additional documents drafted as well.

Durable power of attorney for finances. Should you become incapacitated through illness or injury, this document names an agent to make financial decisions on your behalf. Typically, you will name your spouse, but also name a successor agent in case your agent is unable or unwilling to fulfill his or her duties. Your agent would have the right to pay your bills, deal with insurance companies on your behalf, manage investments, and make other financial decisions.

Durable power of attorney for healthcare. This document names someone to make decisions for you about your healthcare, such as whether to start or stop treatment. This document is also known as a healthcare proxy.

Living will. Imagine you have been in an accident and are being kept alive by a respirator. The doctors look to the person named on your healthcare power of attorney document for a decision about continuing this course of action. Would you want to put him or her in that difficult position? Probably not, and yet just 29 percent of adults have specified what they would want done in that situation via a living will.[2]

A living will goes further than a durable power of attorney for healthcare, enabling you to specify how much care you would want if you were terminally ill or injured. Some states combine the living will and the durable power of attorney for healthcare on the same form.

Health Insurance Portability and Accountability Act (HIPAA) release form. This form is relatively new. It names a representative who may access your medical records that are on file and also receive medical information from medical providers who are treating you. Typically, on your HIPAA release form you will name the same person named in your durable power of attorney for healthcare document, but you can name more than one person.

Do You Need an Attorney?

There are numerous inexpensive software packages and online services you could use to prepare the documents we've been discussing. However, these documents are too important to leave anything to chance, so use an attorney. Depending on the complexity of your situation and the attorney you choose, a package including all of these documents typically will cost between $500 and $2,000. To find a good estate planning attorney, ask friends for referrals or do a search at www.wealthcounsel.com.

☐ CONSIDER A TRUST

When you are young, don't have kids, and don't have a lot of assets, having the set of documents we just discussed should be enough. However, as you have children and build more wealth, a trust may be in order. While you are both living, you make decisions about the trust together. If one dies, the other takes over. You also name someone who is legally bound to carry out your wishes in the event of both of your deaths.

Benefits of Having a Trust

Such a document will typically cost between $1,000 and $3,000, but it can be well worth it because a trust can do some things that a will cannot.

A trust can keep your estate out of probate. Probate often takes at least a year to complete, costs between 2 and 8 percent of the total value of the probate estate, delays the distribution of your estate to your heirs, and makes information about your estate public record. A trust will help you avoid all that.

A trust gives you more control. It can be a bad idea to leave a lot of money to a young adult child. If your state does not allow you to use a will to dictate when your children would receive their inheritance, you can do so with a trust, perhaps staggering the payout with half given when they reach age thirty and the other half at thirty-five. You can even arrange for someone else to manage the inheritance for them and approve spending decisions, or you can slowly transition your children into management of the trust by permitting them to become co-trustees at a certain age and sole trustees sometime later. You can also place restrictions on how the money may be used.

A trust can eliminate or reduce estate taxes. Estate tax laws governing how much of an estate can pass to heirs without tax change frequently. If your estate is large enough to be subject to estate taxes (see my website for the latest thresholds), a trust can help direct more of your assets to your heirs or chosen charities and less to the government.

Types of Trusts

A revocable living trust is the most common type and is mostly for people who want to keep their estate out of probate and control when children can receive their inheritance. Typically, you transfer assets into your trust or name the trust as the beneficiary on various assets and financial accounts, but your attorney will guide you through the details of this process. You'll want to talk with him or her about whether to name the trust as the secondary beneficiary of a tax-advantaged retirement account, as there are some important implications to your choice.

A revocable living trust can help married couples reduce their estate taxes in some cases by doubling the amount they can pass on free of taxes. For larger estates, talk with an experienced estate planning attorney to explore the pros and cons of other trusts.

How Prepared Are Your Parents?

As uncomfortable as the conversation may be, each of you should ask your parents about their estate plan. Do they have wills? Do they have a trust? Having to be involved in a time-consuming probate case after they die will only multiply your grief. If you are at a stage of life when you have young kids or are establishing your career, this is an especially bad time to have to get involved in a probate case.

☐ UPDATE YOUR VOTER REGISTRATION

To determine how to update your name and address, do an Internet search on the name of your state and "Update voter registration."

☐ CHOOSE YOUR INCOME TAX FILING STATUS

For income tax purposes, your marital status on the last day of the year determines your marital status for the entire year. Still, being married doesn't force you into a certain filing status. You have a choice between "married filing jointly" and "married filing separately."

It is almost always best for married couples to file jointly. That's because the income thresholds that move you into more costly tax brackets are higher when earnings are combined than when they're separate. For example, let's say one of you has an adjusted gross income (AGI) of $85,000 and the other $50,000. As single people, the one with the AGI of $85,000 would be in the 28 percent bracket (as of 2010) and the one at $50,000 would be in the 25 percent bracket. But once you're married, if you file jointly, your combined $135,000 AGI will put you in the 25 percent bracket.

Another drawback of filing separately is that doing so will make you ineligible for many tax credits and deductions, such as the child and dependent care credits, the adoption credit, education credits, the earned income tax credit, and the student loan interest deduction. If you are receiving Social Security benefits or bond interest, more of that money may become taxable. Plus, filing separately will lower the income threshold for making tax-deductible contributions to an IRA, and you won't be allowed to convert a traditional IRA to a Roth IRA.

Still, there are some situations in which you may benefit by using the "married filing separately" status. One example is if one of you has a significantly lower income than the other and a lot of eligible itemized deductions, such as medical expenses that are higher than 7.5 percent of your AGI, uninsured property-casualty losses that exceed 10 percent of your AGI, or miscellaneous deductions greater than 2 percent of AGI (such as union dues, certain legal fees, investment expenses, or non-reimbursed business expenses). By filing separately, the spouse with the lower income has a better chance of qualifying for such deductions, which may reduce his or her taxable income and hence the amount to be paid in taxes.

It also may make sense to file separately if just one of you has student loan debt and would like to utilize the income-based repayment plan (discussed in chapter 9). If you file jointly, your monthly payments will be capped at 15 percent of your joint income. However, if you file separately, your payments will be based on only the income of the person who holds the loan, which will leave you with a lower payment.

If you think any of these scenarios may apply to you, figure your taxes both ways—married filing jointly and married filing separately—to see which option makes the most financial sense.

....

Help for Do-It-Yourself Filers

If you do your own taxes using a software package or online service, some make it easy to determine which filing status makes the most sense for you.

TurboTax offers a "What-If Worksheet" that enables you to click a button to create a "married filing jointly" versus "married filing separately" analysis. In "Forms" mode, the "What-If Worksheet" can be found down toward the bottom of the list.

TaxACT Online Deluxe offers a "Joint Versus Separate Report." After entering your federal tax information, a click of a button generates the report telling you which status will enable you to pay the least amount of income tax.

....

Keep in mind, if you decide to file separately, either you both need to itemize or you both need to take the standard deduction.

In community property states, once you're married, your total income and deductions are split fifty-fifty for income tax purposes. There is usually no advantage to filing separately in such states.

For more information on the pros and cons of filing jointly and separately, search for "IRS Publication 501" at www.irs.gov. Publication 555 has more information about community property states.

TAKE IT A STEP AT A TIME

Please don't be overwhelmed by the number of items in this chapter. Just take each item one at a time. Put one on your to-do list each week or every other week, and soon you'll have all of these nitty-gritty details handled. But don't put them off. While they certainly aren't the most romantic aspects of marriage, they are important in helping you build a strong financial foundation.

TAKE ACTION

What to Do

Go through the list of items in this chapter, decide who will handle each task, and schedule the tasks in your calendars.

What to Discuss

- Do you know a good attorney who could draft a will for you? If not, ask friends for referrals.
- If you own property, do you know a good attorney who could help you with any title changes you may need to make?
- How will you file your income taxes? Will one of you do the work or will you use an accountant?

CHAPTER 17

GET ORGANIZED

Everything should be done in a fitting and orderly way.

1 CORINTHIANS 14:40

Anything that does not belong where it is is an "open loop" pulling on your attention.

DAVID ALLEN, AUTHOR OF GETTING THINGS DONE

JUST ABOUT EVERY DAY it seems the postal carrier brings bills, bank or brokerage account statements, and other types of financial paperwork to your home. Don't let it pile up on the counter. That's a recipe for paying bills late and driving your neatnik spouse crazy. Here's how to organize your financial documents.

CHOOSE A BILL-PAYING SYSTEM

If you lose your keys, you might be late for an appointment. But if you misplace a bill and end up paying it late, you could end up hurting your credit score, which can hurt everything from your employment prospects to your mortgage rate. Here's how to make sure you pay your bills on time.

<185>

Option 1. As soon as one bill comes in, pay it and then file the statement as described in the upcoming section.

Option 2. Set up a dedicated place where you stack bills with the one due the soonest on top, and make a note in your calendar as to when to pay the bill. Remember, paying bills late has the greatest negative impact on your credit score (apart from bankruptcy or foreclosure), so put the bill payment date (at least five days before the due date) on your calendar and also sign up for e-mail alerts reminding you about your bill due dates. Once the bill has been paid, file the statement.

Option 3. Sign up for electronic statements and pay all bills online. Jude and I rarely write checks for regular bills. While we still receive some statements through the mail, we're transitioning more of them to electronic bills to cut down on paperwork.

STORE STATEMENTS AND RECEIPTS

Dedicate one drawer of an easily accessible file cabinet for your day-to-day financial records (we'll discuss long-term storage later in the book). Create hanging file folders for the following financial categories listed in bold, and then add regular file folders within each one as described. If you receive electronic statements instead of paper ones for any of the following categories or subcategories, use your Internet browser to set up a financial records favorites or bookmark folder containing each company's website.

- **Income**. Put pay stubs here. If you both work, insert a separate regular file folder into the hanging folder for each of you. At the end of each year, toss your pay stubs and put the year-end W-2s in an Income Tax folder (which you will then move to long-term storage after you file your taxes).
- **Generosity**. Insert one regular file folder for each organization you support. At the end of the year, put year-end giving statements in your Income Tax folder and toss any quarterly or semiannual statements.

- **Banks/brokerage**. Use individual regular file folders for checking, savings, and investment accounts, such as retirement and college investment accounts like a 529 plan.

  You can toss deposit or ATM receipts as soon as you reconcile them with your monthly bank statement and budget. Except for the year-end tax documents, which should be kept in your Income Tax folder, you can get rid of monthly bank and investment statements at the end of each year.

  After filing your income taxes, take year-end investment statements out of your Income Tax folder and put them in an Investments folder you keep in long-term at-home storage until you no longer have the investments.

- **Debts**. Use a regular file folder for each credit card, vehicle, or student loan and any other debt. At the end of each year, you can toss most monthly statements unless you need them to serve as receipts for deductions (move such bills to your Income Tax folder) or warranties (keep in a Warranties/Returns folder in long-term storage).

- **Expenses**. Because there are so many expense categories, use hanging file folders for each of the categories listed below in italics. Then add regular folders where recommended. You don't need to keep receipts for every expense you have. For example, there's no reason to keep receipts for gasoline unless you can get reimbursed for the expense. However, it's a good idea to keep your receipts for the categories listed in alphabetical order below.

  - *Business expenses.* Keep receipts for any expense for which you could get reimbursed, either out of your own business account if you are self-employed or from your employer. After reimbursing yourself for such expenses, transfer these receipts along with your expense reimbursement report to your Income Tax folder if you are self-employed.

  - *Entertainment.* Use regular file folders for cable or satellite television subscriptions, magazine or newspaper subscriptions, health club memberships, and pets (mostly for veterinarian-related paperwork). Most of these documents can be tossed at the end of the year unless you need them for income tax purposes.

- *Health.* Insert regular file folders labeled Medical Insurance, Dental Insurance, Disability Insurance, and Life Insurance. If these premiums are deducted from your paycheck, use the folder for other related paperwork such as statements related to office visits. If you pay these premiums directly, you may want two folders for each type of insurance—one to hold premium statements, the other to hold paperwork related to office visits.

  At the end of the year, you can toss premium statements. Transfer paperwork related to office visits to your long-term financial records storage cabinet. Keep the actual policies in your long-term storage cabinet.

- *Home.* Use regular file folders for your mortgage or rent statements, property tax statements, and homeowners or renters insurance statements and claims (keep the policies in long-term storage).

  At the end of the year, you can throw away mortgage or rent statements as well as insurance premium statements, but be sure to put year-end mortgage tax documents in your Income Tax folder. Transfer your property tax statements to your Income Tax folder as well, and transfer any insurance claim-related paperwork to your long-term storage cabinet.

- *Home maintenance.* Keep receipts for home maintenance–related items. If you sell your home, the future buyer may be interested in these records. You can transfer them to long-term storage at the end of the year. Receipts for maintenance items you may need to return should be kept in your Warranties/Returns folder (in long-term storage). Receipts for energy improvements, which may provide a tax credit, should be kept in your Income Tax folder.

- *Household/personal.* Use a Furniture/Household regular file folder to store receipts for furniture or other household items, or keep them in your Warranties/Returns folder if they are under warranty. If your kids are in private school, use a regular Education file folder so you can keep related receipts or other paperwork. Everything in this category can be tossed at the end of the year.

- *Income tax.* Place all forms, receipts, or other documents related to each year's filing here. Keep this hanging folder in your day-to-day financial records drawer even after the end of the current year so you can add year-end bank and brokerage account statements that usually arrive during the first quarter of the new year. After filing your taxes, put your copies of all related forms in your long-term at-home financial records storage cabinet, where income tax records need to be kept for seven years.

- *Professional services.* Use regular file folders for bills from professionals you use, such as an accountant or lawyer. Billing statements can be tossed at the end of the year unless they provide a tax deduction, in which case they should be transferred to your Income Tax folder.

- *Transportation.* Use regular file folders for vehicle insurance, maintenance, and licenses/fees. Remember, vehicle loan documents go in a Vehicle Loan regular file folder within the Debts hanging folder.

  At the end of the year, transfer vehicle maintenance records to your long-term financial records storage cabinet. When you sell your vehicle, the new owner may want those records. License and fee payment records can be tossed at the end of the year. Keep the vehicle license and registration in the glove compartment.

- *Utilities*. Keep a regular file folder for each utility, such as electric, gas, water, garbage, home phone/Internet, and cell phone. Utility bills can be tossed after you get each new bill unless you need them for income tax purposes.

....

How to Dispose of Old Financial Records

As a protection against identity theft, shred all financial documents before throwing them away. Invest in a good crosscut shredder.

....

WHAT TO KEEP AT HOME IN LONG-TERM STORAGE

Maintain a separate financial records storage file cabinet somewhere else in your house where you will transfer at the end of the year some of the paperwork listed in the previous section.

Documents you should keep locked in this file cabinet include:

- Originals of estate planning documents such as wills, trusts, powers of attorney, living wills (Make sure your attorney has copies of all such documents as well. Your executor, guardians, and/or trustee should also have a copy of your wills and trust.)
- Income tax records from the previous seven years
- Year-end investment account statements (Keep these for as long as you own the investments.)
- Health, home, and vehicle insurance policies (Keep these until you get updated policies.)
- Employer benefit plan updates
- Passports
- Social Security statements (If you don't receive a statement each year, you can request it at www.socialsecurity.gov. Keep

your most recent statement until you get a new one.)

- Warranties/returns (It's easy to lose warranty paperwork and receipts for items you might want to return. Get in the habit of putting these papers in a folder, and it will save you a lot of time and potentially some money down the road.)
- An "If I Die" list of all online accounts and passwords, investment accounts with account numbers, bank accounts with account numbers, insurance policy numbers, credit cards with numbers, and funeral/burial instructions

WHAT TO KEEP IN A SAFE-DEPOSIT BOX

The following are best stored in a safe-deposit box:

- Copies of estate planning documents, such as wills, trusts, powers of attorney, living wills
- Originals of life insurance policies
- Birth, marriage, and death certificates
- Social Security cards
- Original deeds, titles, mortgages, other loans, leases, and other contracts
- Stocks, bonds, and certificates of deposit
- Other valuables such as jewelry, medals, rare stamps, or other collectibles
- Negatives for irreplaceable photos
- Videos or pictures of your home's contents for insurance purposes
- Adoption and custody papers

It will take a little bit of time to set up your financial records management system, but once you do, it will take relatively little time to keep it maintained. As you get older, your lives are likely to grow in complexity. As they do, you will be glad to have set up this system from the start of your marriage.

START SMART

Setting up a smooth-running bill payment system and organizing your files at the start of your marriage will pay great dividends. You'll pay your bills on time, know where to find documents when you need them, and avoid filling your basement with boxes of unneeded paperwork.

TAKE ACTION

What to Do
Decide who will pay the bills and set up your financial document filing system.

What to Discuss
- Which one of you has more natural organizational strengths?
- Which of your bills will you pay online? Will you set up any to be paid automatically?
- Where will you keep your day-to-day financial files?
- Where will you keep your long-term financial files?
- Will you get a safe-deposit box? If so, at what bank or credit union?

CHAPTER 18

WHAT IT'S ALL ABOUT

Everything you were taught can be put into a few words:
Respect and obey God! This is what life is all about.

ECCLESIASTES 12:13 (CEV)

I am nothing special; just a common man with common
thoughts, and I've led a common life. There are no monuments
dedicated to me and my name will soon be forgotten. But in
one respect I have succeeded as gloriously as anyone who's ever
lived: I've loved another with all my heart and soul; and to me,
this has always been enough.

DUKE, *THE NOTEBOOK*

TODAY, ANSWERS TO MOST financial questions are readily available. With the click of a button, you can find advice about getting out of debt, building savings, investing wisely, and getting good deals. Yet there seems to be no end to the number of people who struggle to get the money thing right. The drift of life seems to be toward too much debt, too little savings, and more than enough financial stress.

When I went through my financial crash and burn, I thought my main problem was that I lacked knowledge. Clearly, I had a lot to learn about saving, investing, spending wisely, and debt. However, after committing my life to Christ and reading what the Bible has to say about money and life, I had one of those lightbulb moments. I saw clearly that wise money management does, indeed, require knowledge. But before we can put that knowledge to productive use, we need to understand who we are and what our lives are all about. The parable of the talents opened my eyes to a new perspective on money.

In the opening verses of the parable, Jesus explains what our relationships with God and money are to be:

> It will be like a man going on a journey, who called his servants and entrusted his property to them. To one he gave five talents of money, to another two talents, and to another one talent, each according to his ability. Then he went on his journey. (Matthew 25:14-15)

God is the property owner in this story. He owns everything—our money, cars, computers, abilities, relationships, and even our lives (see Genesis 1:1–2:3 and Psalm 50:9-12). He has generously entrusted us with the responsibility—the opportunity, really—to manage all of it in a way that is consistent with the purposes for which he designed us.

When I got this, it began to change everything about how I viewed and used money. I became more grateful and less demanding. I began to loosen the tight grip with which I held on to the things of this world. I understood in a new way what the Bible means when it says that those who place their faith in Christ become "a new creation; the old has gone, the new has come!" (2 Corinthians 5:17).

Financially, the old that has gone is our consumer identity, where what's mine is mine. The new that has come is our steward or manager identity, where we know that everything in our possession actually belongs to God. Once I understood that I am a manager of God's resources instead of an owner, or even worse, a consumer, I began to understand the purpose of my life. And by understanding the purpose of my life, I understood for the first time the purpose of money.

LIFE PURPOSE #1: LOVE GOD

When Jesus was asked what's most important in life, he said, "Love the Lord your God with all your heart and with all your soul and with all your mind" (Matthew 22:37). What does that look like financially?

Tactically, it means following the action steps described in part 2 of this book: Use a plan to guide your finances; work as if working for the Lord; give generously to help spread the gospel, alleviate the suffering of the poor, and support those who teach God's Word; save adequately; avoid the bondage of debt; maintain a good name by managing your credit score; invest patiently; anticipate danger by building walls of protection; and spend wisely. But it's more than that. You could prioritize your use of money that way and still be doing so for your own purposes.

Jesus was interested in more than the strategic execution of God-honoring principles; he was interested in people's hearts. That's why he often took letter-of-the-law Old Testament teachings and broadened them to spirit-of-the-law, heart-based teachings.

Loving God financially involves cultivating these habits of the heart: contentment, gratitude, patience, and trust.

Contentment. If we felt content, all those new-and-improved televisions, teapots, and tennis rackets would just gather dust in the stores. Because most businesses couldn't survive widespread satisfaction, marketers do all they can to foster discontentment, and if they win, the ramifications go far beyond our bank balance.

Researchers have found that materialistic couples, those who base much of their happiness and self-worth on the material possessions they accumulate, are more likely to experience financial problems and marital conflict. No matter how much they earn, these husbands and wives never feel as though they have enough money.[1]

One of the best ways to jump off the treadmill of want-buy-want is to practice the next heart habit.

Gratitude. When someone gives you a gift, what do you say?

"Thank you," right? Because everything we have is a gift from God, how often do you thank him for your stuff? Think of something you own that you'd like to replace. Maybe a well-worn couch or ten-year-old car. Thank God for it. Practice thanking God for *all* the stuff you own, even the stuff you don't like, and see what happens. My guess is that you will start feeling more content.

Patience. One of the most compelling studies into the power of patience was done at Stanford University in the late 1960s. One at a time, hundreds of four-year-olds were taken into a room with a researcher. The children were told that the researcher was about to leave and that they had two choices: Either they could eat one treat such as a marshmallow right away, or if they could wait for an unspecified period of time until the researcher returned, they could have two marshmallows.

A few kids couldn't wait at all. Before the researcher had even finished the instructions, one marshmallow was gone. The majority of kids held out for an average of three minutes. But about 30 percent were able to resist temptation, waiting the full fifteen minutes the researcher was gone in order to get the better reward.

Years later, when the children in the experiment were in high school, lead researcher Walter Mischel followed up with them and found startling differences between the kids who could wait and those who could not. The children who could hold out for both marshmallows were found to be more confident, effective, self-assertive, and dependable. They were better able to cope with the frustrations of life, less likely to struggle with stress, more likely to embrace challenges, and still able to delay gratification in pursuit of their goals.

The "two marshmallow" kids also scored an average of 210 points higher on their SATs than the "one marshmallow" kids.[2]

It is the lack of the ability to delay gratification that lands so many people in financial hot water. For some, the constant chatter of marketing messages promoting higher-tech televisions, cooler cars, and more hip clothing makes the temptation to overspend a daily struggle.

The good news is that we each have the ability to resist temptation.

In 1 Corinthians 10:13, we read, "No temptation has seized you except what is common to man. And God is faithful; he will not let you be tempted beyond what you can bear. But when you are tempted, he will also provide a way out so that you can stand up under it."

The ultimate "way out" is the recognition that our deepest longings will not be fulfilled on this side of heaven. That's not bad news; it's good news. It fosters patience by helping us stop looking to material things to deliver what they are incapable of delivering. It frees us to enjoy them for what they are: good gifts from God, but not the basis of our identity, security, or ultimate happiness. As John Eldredge puts it, we express our longing for God best when we "have the patience to enjoy what there is now to enjoy, while waiting with eager anticipation for the feast to come."[3]

Trust. As managers of God's resources, we have much to do. There's planning, earning, giving, saving, investing, and spending. But we all face adversity at some point where our best efforts fall short. A job doesn't work out, a medical report comes back with bad news, and worse. We can plan for some of life's disasters with insurance and an emergency fund, but we can't plan for all of them.

That's where trust comes in. The Bible reminds us time and again to cast our cares on God (see 1 Peter 5:7) and that for those who love him, he has our backs. His timing is often different than our preferred timing, but he promises—*promises*—to provide for us (see Matthew 6:25-34).

LIFE PURPOSE #2: LOVE PEOPLE

Right after explaining the first purpose of our lives, Jesus explained the second purpose: "Love your neighbor as yourself" (Matthew 22:39). When you're married, of course, the first person you are to love well is your spouse.

You probably don't need a reminder at this point to love your spouse, but eventually you will. Every healthy relationship involves conflict. In fact, psychologist John Gottman, who has spent more than twenty years studying what makes marriages last, believes that "fighting . . . can be one of the healthiest things a couple can do for their relationship (indeed, how you fight is one of the most telling ways to diagnose the health of your marriage)."[4]

Here are some tips for how to successfully work through the conflict.

Complain, don't criticize. If you're the one raising the issue, be sure to focus on the behavior, not the other person's character. An example of a complaint is "You overspent your clothing budget again this month." It becomes criticism when you blame or make a personal attack or accusation by adding a comment such as "That was really selfish of you."

Avoid contempt. Even worse than criticism, you move into contempt when you intend to insult or psychologically abuse your partner. An example: "What's the matter with you? Don't you ever think before you spend?"

Listen well. When you're on the receiving end of the complaint, focus first on listening. As James said, "Everyone should be quick to listen, slow to speak and slow to become angry" (James 1:19). Rather than following your instinct to come up with a quick response, it's an honoring and validating step to focus on what the other person has to say, asking clarifying questions and mirroring back what you hear.

Speak nondefensively. Defensiveness, which includes denying responsibility and making excuses, only turns up the heat on arguments. When she says, "I think you're spending too much on golf," it won't help to respond with a stormy, "I *have to* spend sixty dollars whenever I play; that's how much it costs." Try this instead: "Well, let's take a look at our budget and see how much I've spent this month compared to the golf budget we both agreed on. If I've spent too much this month, I'll make up for it next month by finding some less expensive places to play."

Stay with it. Gottman says that men especially are likely to check out of an argument. Even if they don't walk away, they may bail out of the conversation by responding with a stony silence. Not a good idea.

Gottman has drawn two simple, powerful conclusions from his years of studying what makes for a healthy marriage. The first is a straightforward mathematical formula: "You must have five times as many positive as negative moments together if your marriage is to be stable."[5] The second is this: "Most couples I've worked with over the years really wanted just two things from their marriage—love and respect."[6] This second conclusion comes straight from the pages of Scripture: "Each one of you also must love his wife as he loves himself, and the wife must respect her husband" (Ephesians 5:33).

One day while reading those verses from Ephesians, the passage came alive for Emerson Eggerichs as never before. As a pastor with twenty years of experience, two master's degrees, and a PhD, he knew a thing or two about the Bible and had counseled many couples. However, that day Eggerichs saw with fresh eyes that a woman's primary need is love and a man's primary need is respect. If she doesn't feel loved, a woman will naturally react to her husband without respect, and without respect, a man will naturally react to his wife without love. That gives rise to what Eggerichs calls "The Crazy Cycle."[7]

How to break out of it? A husband is called to love his wife, even when she's being disrespectful, and a wife is called to respect her husband, even when he's being unloving. That's not easy, but it's amazingly powerful.

As I thought about Ephesians 5:33, it made me wonder about the implications for how husbands and wives use money, especially because finances are one of the most contentious issues in marriage. So I asked Jude what I do financially that makes her feel loved. Then I thought about what she does financially that makes me feel respected. Just bringing it up led to an enjoyable and encouraging conversation. It gave each of us a new appreciation for things the other does that we often take for granted.

She said that knowing I'm managing the details of our budget, making sure we have adequate insurance, taking the initiative to think about and plan for future needs, and generally keeping an eye on our finances makes her feel loved. Okay, she also remembered feeling loved when I uncharacteristically gave her a present that she knew exceeded our gift budget!

I said I feel respected when she reminds our kids in front of me how hard I work for our family. I also feel respected when she finds creative ways to stretch our food and clothing budgets.

When I posed these questions to readers of my blog, one person initially responded that she feels loved when her husband talks with her about large purchase decisions in advance. Doing so makes her feel like a partner in the decision, she explained, not an onlooker. But then she thought about it some more and wrote again:

> You really got me to thinking. It's not a one-way street. I want to feel loved, so I ask for being kept in the loop in financial decisions. But as I considered your question, I began to realize how very, very disrespectful I have behaved toward my husband in our finances, not even consulting him on decisions about spending with my cavalier attitude of "After all, I work and earn a paycheck too!" I had to pray and ask God's forgiveness this morning for my bad behavior as I thought about the dollars I have racked up in credit card debt. I recently received a small inheritance and was reticent to use it to pay off that debt. Now I see the need to do just that. Then I need to ask my husband's forgiveness next. That will be the hardest part. Thanks for the prodding.

Men and women both need love and respect, but men especially thrive on respect; women especially thrive on love. It's just how God made us. Finding out what you do or could do financially to meet this need in your spouse will help your marriage.

LIFE PURPOSE #3: MAKE A DIFFERENCE

Our culture encourages us to pursue lives of competition, striving to have more than we have now and more than others have. We naturally play the comparison game, noticing what our neighbors and coworkers are driving, wearing, and planning for this year's vacation. We base our happiness on how we stand in relation to others.

But that's not the life for which we were made. We were not designed for competition; we were designed for contribution. As the Bible says, "Each one should use whatever gift he has received to serve others" (1 Peter 4:10).

Both of you have been given gifts, talents, and passions. You'll know the contribution God has designed you for when you start talking in an animated way about something you're committed to doing with your life. Your arms start waving, you lean forward, your voice comes alive, and time passes quickly.

What is that for you? What difference do you long to make with your life? Ideally, you will each be able to answer that question and you will support the other in the pursuit of that contribution. Just as ideally, you will be able to answer that question as a couple. What contribution is God calling you to make together?

One of my primary passions is to help transform people's lives by teaching the practical application of God's timeless truths about money. Jude is a full partner in this work, sharing the vision and helping in its fulfillment by helping me hone the content of my writing and workshops, sometimes teaching with me, and in countless other ways. For several years, she has had a vision of having me teach half-day Money & Marriage workshops in cities throughout the country. It is a vision that is starting to come together due in large part to her persistence in championing the idea.

One of Jude's primary passions is parenthood. Of course, it's one of mine, too, so we both make sacrifices in order to be able to have her be home with our young kids full-time.

Many two-income couples with kids tell me they would love to figure out a way to make it as a one-income household. They want to be more involved in their kids' lives, yet they can't imagine how that could possibly work. It *can* work, and if this is a passionate desire of yours, you have to make it work.

Question all of your financial decisions, starting with your biggest expense, which is housing for most people. I know, it's a crazy thought to consider moving. It's disruptive, to say the least. But if it's what it will take to do what God has put on your heart to do, it will be one of the most rewarding decisions of your life.

If you don't know what contribution you were designed for, please keep looking. Keep praying.

MY PRAYER FOR YOU

As I continued reading the parable of the talents, I found myself lingering over these words: "After a long time the master of those servants returned and settled accounts with them" (Matthew 25:19). One day the Master will, indeed, return. And he will settle accounts with us, taking stock of what we have done with all he generously entrusted to us.

In the parable, the master had these strong words of affirmation for each of the two servants who had made something more of what had been entrusted to them: "Well done, good and faithful servant! You have been faithful with a few things; I will put you in charge of many things. Come and share your master's happiness!" (Matthew 25:21). To the one who hid what had been entrusted to him, the master had harsh words of rebuke.

My prayer for you is that you will use money in a way that brings great glory to God; shows love to the people in your lives, starting with each other; and enables you to use the talents and passions God has uniquely given you to make the contribution for which you were uniquely designed. If you arrange your finances around these three God-given purposes, your marriage will be richly blessed, and I believe that one day you will hear these words: "Well done, good and faithful servants!"

ACKNOWLEDGMENTS

IT TAKES A VILLAGE to write a book, and in this case it took a mighty big village. While any errors in this book are my responsibility alone, any help this book provides is due in large part to the contributions of the following people.

To the many financial, legal, and real estate professionals I talked with, thank you for selflessly sharing your time and expertise and for your patience with my many questions. These people include: David Estridge, Hope Smith, and Barbara Dye at Christian Community Credit Union; Matt Carothers at Northwestern Mutual; CPA Steve Zoller; Michelle Bobart with Guaranteed Rate; attorneys Amy Bakker Baty, Stephen Bloom, Rick Boonstra, David Hoy, Natalia Kabbe, Rodney and Matt Piercey, and William Sheffer; financial advisors Tim Mohns and Tom Vislisel; financial advisor and author Jerry Tuma; Craig Watts at Fair Isaac Corporation; and John Ulzheimer of Credit.com.

To Brad Brestel and Chris Goulard, thank you for your guidance and help in tracking down answers to several key questions.

To Dustin Riechmann of EngagedMarriage.com, thank you for allowing me to ask questions of your readers and for reviewing the manuscript.

To everyone who shared part of your story with me, thank you for

<203>

your willingness to allow the lessons you have learned to help others.

To Park Community Church Family Pastor Bill Meier and former Park Family Pastor Keith Wilson, thank you for allowing me to test this material through many premarital workshops.

To everyone at NavPress, it's a privilege to be associated with such an outstanding publisher. In particular, thank you, Mike Miller, for the opportunity to continue partnering with you; thank you, Kris Wallen, for handling more details on this project than seemed humanly possible, and for handling them so well; and thank you, Arvid Wallen, for your creativity.

To Liz Heaney, you are a world-class editor and so much more. Thank you for being a trusted advisor and friend.

To Erik Wolgemuth, thank you for your always-sound business advice, prayers, and friendship.

To Dave Briggs and Jerry and Sandy Wiseman, thank you for holding your wisdom with open hands. Your feedback on the manuscript was invaluable.

To Dick Towner, much of what I know about biblical money management has come from your teaching and example. Thank you for your mentoring and friendship.

To the many family members and friends who encouraged and prayed for me while I wrote, thank you. They include David Bell, Jim and Kirsten Bell, Paul and Sheila Jenkinson, Dwight and Betty Nelson, Bret and Becky Petkus, Wayne Riendeau, Mark Salavitch, Craig and Laurie Steensma, and the women of the Riverside prayer group.

To my children: Jonathan, Andrew, and Annika. How is it that you always seemed to know just when I needed a break from writing to enjoy a good laugh, chase you around the house, or get lost in the wonders of your latest LEGO creation? I am endlessly thankful for the joy of being your dad.

Mostly to my wife, Jude, thank you for your commitment to follow God no matter what the cost. One day this crazy adventure is all going to make sense. For now, I am so thankful to be traveling every twist and turn in the road hand in hand with you. Your love makes all the difference in my life. If I accomplish nothing else, I will breathe my last, happy and grateful to have married well.

Recommended Monthly Spending Guidelines

(One-Person Household)

Annual Gross Income	$30,000		$45,000		$60,000	
Monthly Gross Income	$2,500		$3,750		$5,000	
Giving	$250	10.0%	$375	10.0%	$500	10.0%
Saving/Investing	$250	10.0%	$412	11.0%	$600	12.0%
Consumer Debts	$0	0%	$0	0%	$0	0%
Mortgage/Rent, Taxes, Insurance	$625	25.0%	$919	24.5%	$1,175	23.5%
Maintenance/Utilities	$150	6.0%	$206	5.5%	$250	5.0%
Transportation	$225	9.0%	$262	7.0%	$300	6.0%
Income Taxes	$405	16.2%	$652	17.4%	$915	18.3%
Food	$250	10.0%	$319	8.5%	$350	7.0%
Clothing	$30	1.2%	$75	2.0%	$150	3.0%
Other Household/Personal	$30	1.2%	$75	2.0%	$100	2.0%
Entertainment	$50	2.0%	$94	2.5%	$175	3.5%
Health	$200	8.0%	$300	8.0%	$350	7.0%
Professional Services	$10	0.4%	$38	1.0%	$50	1.0%
Miscellaneous	$25	1.0%	$23	0.6%	$25	0.5%
Discretionary	$0	0%	$0	0%	$60	1.2%
Total	$2,500	100%	$3,750	100%	$5,000	100%

<207>

(One-Person Household)

Annual Gross Income	$75,000		$90,000		$105,000	
Monthly Gross Income	$6,250		$7,500		$8,750	
Giving	$625	10.0%	$750	10.0%	$876	10.0%
Saving/Investing	$813	13.0%	$1,050	14.0%	$1,313	15.0%
Consumer Debts	$0	0%	$0	0%	$0	0%
Mortgage/Rent, Taxes, Insurance	$1,375	22.0%	$1,538	20.5%	$1,706	19.5%
Maintenance/Utilities	$281	4.5%	$315	4.2%	$350	4.0%
Transportation	$300	4.8%	$300	4.0%	$306	3.5%
Income Taxes	$1,256	20.1%	$1,610	21.5%	$1,916	21.9%
Food	$400	6.4%	$405	5.4%	$411	4.7%
Clothing	$200	3.2%	$248	3.3%	$254	2.9%
Other Household/Personal	$156	2.5%	$188	2.5%	$219	2.5%
Entertainment	$250	4.0%	$300	4.0%	$350	4.0%
Health	$356	5.7%	$360	4.8%	$385	4.4%
Professional Services	$50	0.8%	$51	0.7%	$52	0.6%
Miscellaneous	$25	0.4%	$25	0.3%	$26	0.3%
Discretionary	$163	2.6%	$360	4.8%	$586	6.7%
Total	$6,250	100%	$7,500	100%	$8,750	100%

(One-Person Household)

Annual Gross Income	$120,000		$135,000		$150,000	
Monthly Gross Income	$10,000		$11,250		$12,500	
Giving	$1,000	10.0%	$1,125	10.0%	$1,250	10.0%
Saving/Investing	$1,500	15.0%	$1,687	15.0%	$1,875	15.0%
Consumer Debts	$0	0%	$0	0%	$0	0%
Mortgage/Rent, Taxes, Insurance	$1,850	18.5%	$2,025	18.0%	$2,187	17.5%
Maintenance/Utilities	$385	3.85%	$416	3.7%	$437	3.5%
Transportation	$300	3.0%	$304	2.7%	$300	2.4%
Income Taxes	$2,200	22.0%	$2,486	22.1%	$2,788	22.3%
Food	$410	4.1%	$427	3.8%	$425	3.4%
Clothing	$250	2.5%	$248	2.2%	$250	2.0%
Other Household/Personal	$250	2.5%	$281	2.5%	$313	2.5%
Entertainment	$400	4.0%	$450	4.0%	$500	4.0%
Health	$400	4.0%	$405	3.6%	$412	3.3%
Professional Services	$50	0.5%	$55	0.5%	$50	0.4%
Miscellaneous	$25	0.25%	$25	0.2%	$25	0.2%
Discretionary	$980	9.8%	$1,316	11.7%	$1,688	13.5%
Total	$10,000	100%	$11,250	100%	$12,500	100%

(Two-Person Household)

Annual Gross Income	$30,000		$45,000		$60,000	
Monthly Gross Income	$2,500		$3,750		$5,000	
Giving	$250	10.0%	$375	10.0%	$500	10.0%
Saving/Investing	$250	10.0%	$375	10.0%	$550	11.0%
Consumer Debts	$0	0%	$0	0%	$0	0%
Mortgage/Rent, Taxes, Insurance	$625	25.0%	$930	24.8%	$1,215	24.3%
Maintenance/Utilities	$150	6.0%	$203	5.4%	$250	5.0%
Transportation	$213	8.5%	$375	10.0%	$425	8.5%
Income Taxes	$340	13.6%	$570	15.2%	$815	16.3%
Food	$313	12.5%	$375	10.0%	$400	8.0%
Clothing	$37	1.5%	$60	1.6%	$150	3.0%
Other Household/Personal	$40	1.6%	$56	1.5%	$85	1.7%
Entertainment	$30	1.2%	$56	1.5%	$100	2.0%
Health	$225	9.0%	$300	8.0%	$360	7.2%
Professional Services	$15	0.6%	$37	1.0%	$100	2.0%
Miscellaneous	$12	0.5%	$38	1.0%	$50	1.0%
Discretionary	$0	0%	$0	0%	$0	0%
Total	$2,500	100%	$3,750	100%	$5,000	100%

(Two-Person Household)

Annual Gross Income	$75,000		$90,000		$105,000	
Monthly Gross Income	$6,250		$7,500		$8,750	
Giving	$625	10.0%	$750	10.0%	$875	10.0%
Saving/Investing	$781	12.5%	$1,125	15.0%	$1,312	15.0%
Consumer Debts	$0	0%	$0	0%	$0	0%
Mortgage/Rent, Taxes, Insurance	$1,469	23.5%	$1,688	22.5%	$1,925	22.0%
Maintenance/Utilities	$313	5.0%	$375	5.0%	$438	5.0%
Transportation	$450	7.2%	$450	6.0%	$455	5.2%
Income Taxes	$1,069	17.1%	$1,320	17.6%	$1,531	17.5%
Food	$450	7.2%	$450	6.0%	$455	5.2%
Clothing	$206	3.3%	$248	3.3%	$263	3.0%
Other Household/Personal	$125	2.0%	$150	2.0%	$175	2.0%
Entertainment	$187	3.0%	$225	3.0%	$306	3.5%
Health	$425	6.8%	$450	6.0%	$473	5.4%
Professional Services	$100	1.6%	$97	1.3%	$105	1.2%
Miscellaneous	$50	0.8%	$52	0.7%	$52	0.6%
Discretionary	$0	0%	$120	1.6%	$385	4.4%
Total	$6,250	100%	$7,500	100%	$8,750	100%

(Two-Person Household)

Annual Gross Income	\$120,000		\$135,000		\$150,000	
Monthly Gross Income	\$10,000		\$11,250		\$12,500	
Giving	\$1,000	10.0%	\$1,125	10.0%	\$1,250	10.0%
Saving/Investing	\$1,500	15.0%	\$1,688	15.0%	\$1,875	15.0%
Consumer Debts	\$0	0%	\$0	0%	\$0	0%
Mortgage/Rent, Taxes, Insurance	\$2,150	21.5%	\$2,363	21.0%	\$2,563	20.5%
Maintenance/Utilities	\$450	4.5%	\$506	4.5%	\$563	4.5%
Transportation	\$450	4.5%	\$450	4.0%	\$450	3.6%
Income Taxes	\$1,760	17.6%	\$2,019	17.9%	\$2,287	18.3%
Food	\$460	4.6%	\$473	4.2%	\$500	4.0%
Clothing	\$300	3.0%	\$338	3.0%	\$375	3.0%
Other Household/Personal	\$200	2.0%	\$225	2.0%	\$250	2.0%
Entertainment	\$350	3.5%	\$394	3.5%	\$475	3.8%
Health	\$500	5.0%	\$506	4.5%	\$500	4.0%
Professional Services	\$100	1.0%	\$101	0.9%	\$100	0.8%
Miscellaneous	\$50	0.5%	\$50	0.5%	\$50	0.4%
Discretionary	\$730	7.3%	\$1,012	9.0%	\$1,262	10.1%
Total	\$10,000	100%	\$11,250	100%	\$12,500	100%

Recommended
Housing Guidelines

<211>

Recommended Housing Guidelines for a Two-Person Household

Annual Gross Income	$30,000*	$45,000	$60,000	$75,000	$90,000	$105,000	$120,000	$135,000	$150,000
Monthly Gross Income	$2,500	$3,750	$5,000	$6,250	$7,500	$8,750	$10,000	$11,250	$12,500
Home Purchase Price	$106,250	$158,750	$208,125	$252,500	$290,625	$332,500	$372,500	$410,000	$445,625
Total Mortgage (with 20% down payment)	$85,000	$127,000	$166,500	$202,000	$232,500	$266,000	$298,000	$328,000	$356,500
Monthly Mortgage Payment (6%)	$511	$763	$999	$1,210	$1,394	$1,594	$1,785	$1,966	$2,137
Insurance	$29	$42	$52	$60	$66	$71	$75	$78	$79
Taxes	$85	$125	$164	$199	$228	$260	$290	$319	$347
Total of Mortgage/Insurance/Taxes	$625	$930	$1,215	$1,469	$1,688	$1,925	$2,150	$2,363	$2,563
Percentage of Monthly Gross Income	25.0%	24.8%	24.3%	23.5%	22.5%	22.0%	21.5%	21.0%	20.5%

*At the $30,000 income level, a family would probably be better off renting. Without a real estate tax payment, that would enable them to spend nearly $600 per month on an apartment. Plus, they would reduce their risk of having to pay for potentially costly repairs to a home.

NOTES

Chapter 1

1. "The Truth About American Marriage," *Parade Magazine*, September 15, 2008, http://www.parade.com/hot-topics/2008/09/truth-about-american-marriage-poll-results.

2. Jeffrey Dew, "Bank On It: Thrifty Couples Are the Happiest," *The State of Our Unions, Marriage in America 2009: Money & Marriage*, http://www.virginia.edu/marriageproject, 28.

3. Dew, 28.

4. Ramit Sethi, "Gender and Finance" survey, August 24, 2007, http://www.slideshare.net/ramit/iwillteachyoutoberich-survey-on-gender-and-money-with-gender-differences-highlighted, 12.

5. Sethi, 16.

6. Pew Research Center, "Where Men and Women Differ in Following the News," February 6, 2008, http://pewresearch.org/pubs/722/men-women-follow-news.

7. Sethi, 19.

8. Shankar Vedantam, "Salary, Gender and the Social Cost of Haggling," *The Washington Post*, July 30, 2007, http://www.washingtonpost.com/wp-dyn/content/article/2007/07/29/AR2007072900827.html.

9. Pat Regnier and Amanda Gengler, "Men, women . . . and money," *Money Magazine*, March 14, 2006, http://money.cnn.com/2006/03/

<213>

10/pf/marriage_short_moneymag_0604/index.htm.

10. Merrill Lynch Investment Managers news release "When It Comes to Investing, Gender a Strong Influence on Behavior," April 18, 2005, http://www.ml.com/media/47547.pdf.

11. Merrill Lynch Investment Managers news release.

12. Suzanne Miller, "Do Men and Women Think About Money Differently?" *Forbes.com*, March 16, 2010, http://www.forbes.com/2010/03/16/saving-spending-financial-assets-adviser-forbes-woman-net-worth-money-management_2.html.

13. Ohio State University news release "Husbands, Wives Don't Agree on Their Financial Status, Study Finds," May 27, 2003, http://researchnews.osu.edu/archive/famfinan.htm.

14. Sethi, 18.

15. Catherine Rampell, "I Say Spend. You Say No. We're in Love." *New York Times*, 8/15/2009, http://www.nytimes.com/2009/08/16/weekinreview/16rampell.html?_r=2&ref=weekinreview.

16. Kate Ashford, "She's a Saver, He's a Spender," *Money.CNN.com*, August 24, 2006, http://money.cnn.com/2006/08/23/pf/spender_saver.moneymag/index.htm.

17. Fidelity Investments news release "Fidelity Research Finds Couples Make No Progress in Joint Planning and Management of Retirement Finances Despite Historic Market Volitility," June 10, 2009, http://www2.prnewswire.com/mnr/fidelity/38691/.

18. Scott Medintz, "Secrets, Lies and Money," *CNNMoney.com*, April 2005, http://money.cnn.com/pr/subs/magazine_archive/2005/05/LIE.html.

19. Keith Huang, "Most American Couples Discuss Financial Issues, Harris Poll Shows," *Wall Street Journal Online*, March 12, 2007, http://online.wsj.com/article/SB117138226750307290.html.

20. Geoff Williams, "What to do when your spouse admits to $68,000 in credit card debt," *WalletPop*, March 12, 2010, http://www.walletpop.com/blog/2010/03/12/what-to-do-when-your-spouse-admits-to-68-000-in-credit-card-deb/.

21. Aleksandra Todorova, "The Six Financial Mistakes Couples Make," *SmartMoney*, June 11, 2008, http://www.smartmoney .com/personal-finance/marriage-divorce/the-six-financial-mistakes -couples-make-15414/.

22. Medintz.

23. Regnier and Gengler.

24. Matthew 7:24-27.

Chapter 4

1. David Keirsey, *Please Understand Me II* (Del Mar, CA: Prometheus Nemesis Book Company, 1998), 2, 26.

2. Used with permission from Jerry (and Ramona) Tuma, *Smart Money* (Sisters, OR: Multnomah, 1994), 30–31.

3. For a more detailed understanding of how temperament impacts your view and use of money, read Jerry and Ramona Tuma's excellent book *Smart Money* referenced above.

4. Maureen Farrell, "Surviving a Workaholic Spouse," *Forbes.com*, December 20, 2009, http://abcnews.go.com/Business/surviving -workaholic-spouse/story?id=9355694.

5. Nightly Business Report, "What's Your Investment Temperament?" *PBS.org*, http://www.pbs.org/nbr/site/features/special/subdir/ mind_and_money_resource_temperament/.

Chapter 5

1. Dustin Riechmann, "Marriage and Money: Questions for Young Couples," *Engaged Marriage*, March 30, 2010, http://www .engagedmarriage.com/ask-the-community/marriage-and-money -questions-for-young-couples.

2. Matt Bell, "Budget Users Less Likely to Have Financial Fights," February 10, 2010, http://www.mattaboutmoney.com/media/ news-releases/.

3. Christine Larson, "6 Smart Ways to Stop Money Stress in Your Marriage," *Redbook*, http://www.redbookmag.com/money-career/

tips-advice/stop-money-stress.

4. Bell.

5. Bell.

6. "Money? Sex? What couples are fighting about," *CNNMoney.com*, March 14, 2006, http://money.cnn.com/magazines/moneymag/ marriage_money/.

7. Jeffrey Dew, "Bank On It: Thrifty Couples Are the Happiest," *The State of Our Unions, Marriage in America 2009: Money & Marriage*, http://www.virginia.edu/marriageproject, 26–27.

Chapter 6

1. Erin White, "Corporate Tuition Aid Appears to Keep Workers Loyal," *Wall Street Journal*, 5/21/07, B4.

Chapter 7

1. David Myers, *The Pursuit of Happiness* (New York: Morrow, 1992), 194–195.

2. UNICEF news release, http://www.unicef.org/rightsite/sowc/ presscentre.php.

Chapter 8

1. Matt Bell, "Tough Times Call for a Return to the Basics of Wise Money Management," December 21, 2008, http://www .mattaboutmoney.com/media/news-releases/.

Chapter 9

1. Jeffrey Dew, "Bank On It: Thrifty Couples Are the Happiest," *The State of Our Unions, Marriage in America 2009: Money & Marriage*, http://www.virginia.edu/marriageproject, 24–25.

2. Jeffrey Dew, "Debt Change and Marital Satisfaction Change in Recently Married Couples," *Family Relations*, January, 2008, http://findarticles.com/p/articles/mi_7532/is_200801/ai _n32260929/?tag=content;col1, 60–71.

Chapter 11

1. Employee Benefit Research Institute, "2010 Retirement Confidence Survey," http://www.ebri.org/surveys/rcs/2010/.

2. Dan Solin, "Seven Shocking Tips to Boost Your Returns by 400 Percent (or More)," *Daily Finance*, January 1, 2010, http://www .dailyfinance.com/story/dan-solin-seven-shocking-tips-to-boost -your-returns-by-400-or/19274858/.

3. John Bogle, *The Little Book of Common Sense Investing* (Hoboken, NJ: Wiley, 2007), 208.

Chapter 12

1. "How much insurance do you need?" *Consumer Reports*, April 2007, http://www.consumerreports.org/cro/babies-kids/baby -toddler/money-tips-for-new-parents-10-07/how-much-life -insurance-do-you-need/how-much-insurance-do-you-need.htm.

2. The Life and Health Insurance Foundation for Education, "Who Needs Disability Insurance?" http://lifehappens.org/disability -insurance/who-needs-it.

3. National Association of Insurance Commissioners news release "Majority of Americans Unprepared for Financial Impact of Disability, NAIC Survey Shows," February 28, 2007, http://www .naic.org/Releases/2007_docs/insure_u_disability.htm.

4. Ron Lieber, "The Odds of a Disability Are Themselves Odd," *New York Times*, February 5, 2010, http://www.nytime. com/2010/02/06/your-money/life-and-disability-insurance/ 06money.html.

5. Ginger Applegarth, "Disability insurance can save your life," *MSN.com*, August 20, 2008, http://articles.moneycentral.msn .com/Insurance/InsureYourHealth/DisabilityInsuranceCan SaveYourLife.aspx.

Chapter 13

1. www.myfico.com, May 26, 2010.
2. Robert Bernabé, *Mind Your Own Mortgage* (Nashville: Nelson, 2010), 125.

Chapter 15

1. Laura Petrecca, "Prenuptial agreements: Unromantic, but important," *USA TODAY*, March 11, 2010, http://www.usatoday.com/money/perfi/basics/2010-03-08-prenups08_CV_N.htm.

Chapter 16

1. Lawyers.com news release "Lawyers.com Survey Reveals Drop in Estate Planning," February 25, 2010, http://www.lawyers.com/understand-your-legal-issue/press-room/2010-Will-Survey-Press-Release.html.
2. Kim Parker, "Coping with End-Of-Life Decisions," *Pew Research Center*, http://pewresearch.org/pubs/1320/opinion-end-of-life-care-right-to-die-living-will.

Chapter 18

1. Jeffrey Dew, "Bank On It: Thrifty Couples Are the Happiest," *The State of Our Unions, Marriage in America 2009: Money & Marriage*, http://www.virginia.edu/marriageproject, 27.
2. Jonah Lehrer, "Don't! The Secret of Self-Control," *The New Yorker*, May 18, 2009, http://www.newyorker.com/reporting/2009/05/18/090518fa_fact_lehrer.
3. John Eldredge and Brent Curtis, *The Sacred Romance* (Nashville: Nelson, 1997), 199.
4. John Gottman, *Why Marriages Succeed or Fail* (New York: Simon & Schuster, 1994), 15.
5. Gottman, 29.
6. Gottman, 18.
7. Emerson Eggerichs, *Love and Respect* (Nashville: Nelson, 2004), 16.

AUTHOR

MATT BELL is a personal finance writer and speaker and author of *Money, Purpose, Joy* and *Money Strategies for Tough Times.* He speaks at churches, universities, conferences, and other venues throughout the country. Matt has been quoted in *USA Today, U.S. News and World Report,* the *Chicago Tribune,* and *Kiplinger's Personal Finance* magazine and has been a guest on WGN-TV and several nationally syndicated radio talk shows. He holds a master's degree in interdisciplinary studies from DePaul University, where he wrote a thesis about the emergence of America's consumer culture and its influence on people's beliefs and behaviors. Matt lives with his wife and their three young children in the Chicago area. To learn more about his work and subscribe to his blog, go to www.MattAboutMoney.com.

<219>

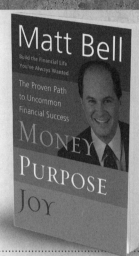